Film Actresses

Volume 13

Jean Harlow

Documentary book

ISBN-13 : 978-1502918413
ISBN-10 : 1502918412

Dtp
and
graphic design

Iacob Adrian

Author statement

The actors and actresses are the the bricks .

The cast and crew are the plaster .

They stand on the foundation created by
producers and writers and directors .

All these people creates the great palace
of the art of film .

Iacob Adrian - 2013

Jean Harlow's
SUMMER
DIET
SECRETS

Use the methods employed by one of the most beautiful stars to improve your health and keep your proper weight during hot weather

by FRANCES KELLUM

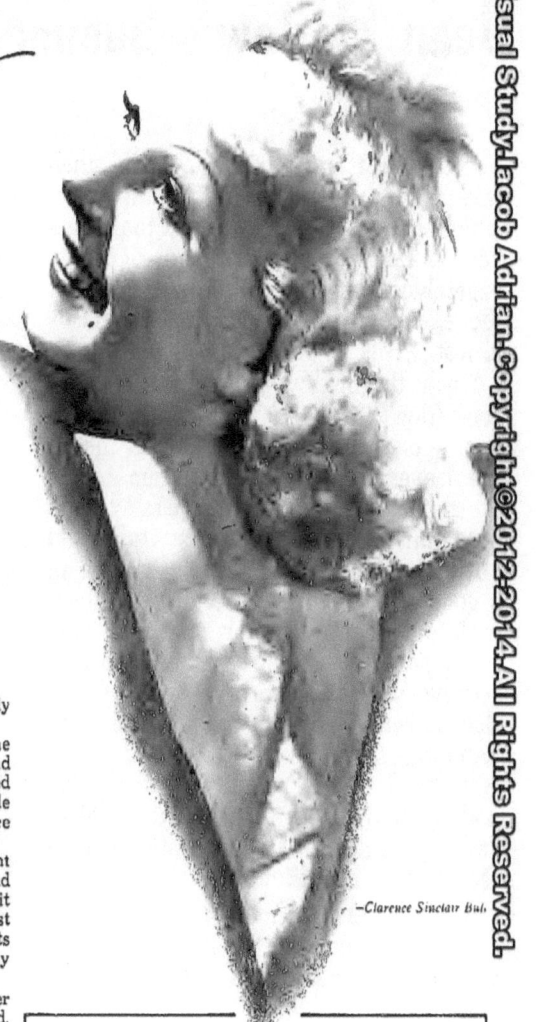

—*Clarence Sinclair Bul.*

D o You Know that you can build up a whole new body for yourself this summer?

Do you know that it's possible, in the midst of the heat and languor and all, to create for yourself the kind of complexion you've dreamed of having? Fine textured skin, smooth as a gardenia petal. Not a single telltale "bump" as you pass your fingers lightly over the surface of your face.

This is no idle, oh-it-never-could-happen-to-me thought of wonder worked by magic. This is *science*. Pure—and quite simple. Medical science. Or rather, that part of it which has to do with the foods we eat. Some of the most famous health specialists in America have told their secrets to Jean Harlow. She was telling us about them one day as we idled in her garden.

"During the winter you naturally have to eat heavier foods that will supply heat for the body," she explained. "But when the warm months come—that's the time to do things to yourself with diet. Out here in Hollywood where we have a semi-tropical climate and most of us are working under blazing lights so much of the time, we have to take special precautions. I've found that out!"

● And here is the first step Jean suggests in the re-building process. It is also the pet secret of one of the most noted beauticians in the world. She prescribes it for every client before she applies any cream or tonic to their face—as the foundation for a series of treatments costing $250! But it's worth $250 and infinitely more to know how to eliminate stored-up poisons in the system . . .

This is called the Seven Day Eliminative Diet. There's nothing stringent or harmful about it. And certainly you don't starve! Begin in the morning by taking a half teaspoonful of vegetable salts—procurable at any health food store—in a glass of hot water. For breakfast drink the juice of three oranges. If you're working, you require extra nourishment and a very soft boiled egg is permitted but no bulky foods.

At eleven drink a glass of tomato juice seasoned with lemon juice. This can easily be taken to your place of

Jean's Two Favorite Hot Weather Suppers

Grapefruit cup
(chilled, diced grapefruit)
Jellied chicken loaf
(see story for recipe)
Radishes, olives, green onions   Hot rolls
Open-faced cherry pie
Iced coffee
* * *
Olives, celery
Chipped dry beef sauté
(cooked with onion in butter)
Stuffed eggs
(small bread and butter sandwiches)
Hot asparagus
(with lemon-butter and paprika)
Camembert cheese   Crackers and honey

Jean Harlow's Summer Diet Secrets

business in a small thermos. For lunch take a large portion of potassium broth, which is considered the best tonic and body builder possible. It's made of whole vegetables, tops and all, so that none of the excellent blood-purifying chemicals is lost. This is the recipe:

Wash thoroughly one bunch of carrots (don't forget to include the green tops!), one bunch of celery (this means the leaves and everything), one bunch of spinach, one bunch of parsley, and one bunch of green onions (tails and all). Cut the vegetables up very fine in a good-sized boiling pot and cover them with four quarts of water. Let this stand for a half hour. Thirty minutes before serving, put the soup on a low light so that it will cook slowly. Season with vegetable salts. To vary it, a little tomato broth can be mixed with it one day and bouillon cubes the next. Taken daily, potassium broth is nature's own recipe for a beautiful skin!

If you haven't time to make it, it comes already prepared in small cans and all you have to do is add the water and seasoning.

Also on the seven day diet, you're allowed to have as large a vegetable salad as you can eat *with French dressing,* and your favorite fruit, fresh or stewed, for luncheon. Jean Harlow's choice at noon is usually a big dish of sliced tomatoes with cottage cheese in the center. There are any number of appetizing salads these days to choose from.

In the middle of the afternoon drink a tall glass of lemonade. For dinner, take as generous an amount of potassium broth again as you can. Also a goodly sized vegetable plate with five or six steamed vegetables and whatever fresh fruit you prefer or a baked apple. In steaming vegetables you not only retain all their best substances, which is thrown away when you boil them, but you add to their flavor and they cook in half the time.

Before retiring, drink another tumbler of hot water with the vegetable salts in it.

A week of this—and you feel like a new person. As a matter of fact you are new because you've built up fresh body tissues. You've alkalized your system so that the bugaboo of summer colds disappears. The heat loses its power to make you so deadly tired. You feel a surprising new energy creeping into you. That's the million dollar secret of the stars!

But, As Jean says, on the *eighth* day don't try to counteract all the good you've accomplished by stuffing with sugars, and roast pork and rich gravies! Be wise. Eat a light meat like lamb or chicken at first. Pork should never be taken in the summer. Eat tasty gelatines —with whipped cream if you like. Ice-cold fruit cups are also one of the most appetizing summer desserts you can have. Prune whip is another.

If you get hungry between meals, the finest thing you can do for your body is to take a lovely big peach or a nice red apple or pear or some grapes—*and a handful of freshly roasted nuts,* and eat them alternately. The chemical action thus produced is like a revivifying tonic in the effect it has on your blood stream.

Sugar on fruit is delicious, of course, but it does create an acid which sometimes causes gastric disturbances and that in turn makes skin eruptions. So if

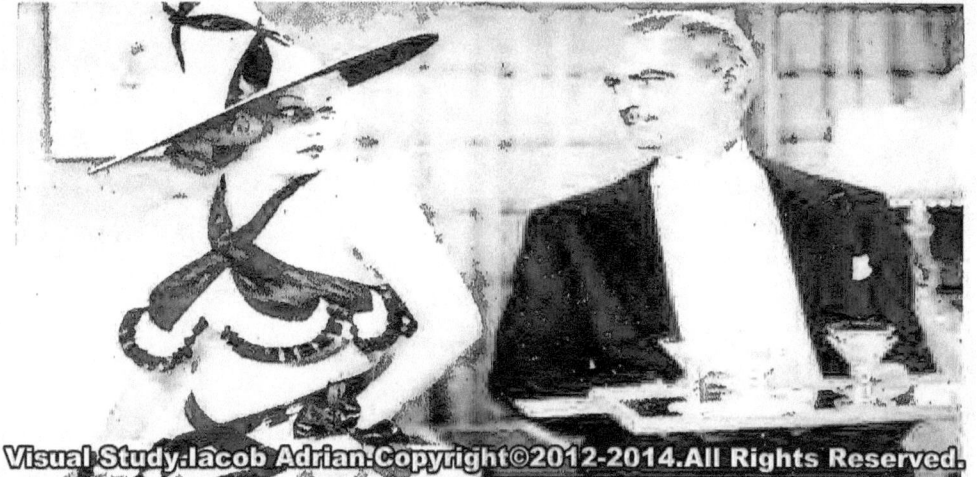

Jean Harlow receives the witheringly pointed comment and stare of—tschk, tschk, how different he looks!—Lionel Barrymore in this advance scene from her picture,
Born to be Kissed

you want to sweeten your fruit, use strained honey.

"I'll tell you what makes a grand hot-weather supper," Jean said. "A grapefruit cup—you know, diced grapefruit that's been chilled. A jellied chicken loaf. Radishes, olives and green onions. Hot rolls. An open-face cherry pie and iced coffee! The jellied chicken loaf is simple to make. You take two level teaspoons of unflavored gelatin and soak it in a ¼ cup of cold water. Dissolve in three cups of hot, well-seasoned chicken broth or canned strained chicken soup. Season with salt and a dash of cayenne. Let it cool. In your mould put about a half inch of the jelly. As it thickens, decorate with sliced stuffed green olives and slices of hard-boiled egg. When solid, put in a layer of chicken, diced, mixed with enough jelly to hold it. Next, one cup of green peas, diced celery and a chopped green pepper, with sufficient jelly to hold. Lastly, as much diced chicken as the remaining jelly will bind. Let each layer harden in the icebox before adding the next one. Unmould on a bed of lettuce and garnish with parsley and sliced tomatoes. Serve with mayonnaise.

"You know what mother used to do when I was little? Appetites have to be coaxed when it's so hot and she'd fix up attractive picnics that we'd have in the back yard. I remember I thought it was great sport to make George Washington white paper caps large enough to put over each dish to keep the flies away! Mother used one of those Dutch ovens to cook our roasts and all so she wouldn't have to heat up the kitchen by lighting the real oven. She'd put a leg of lamb on and when it was three-quarters done, in would go the vegetables—carrots and dry onions and potatoes—and pretty soon the whole dinner would be cooked without any trouble or much heat. She even heated the rolls up in the Dutch oven!

"One of our favorite summer suppers out-of-doors was—and still is—chipped dry beef sauté, that is cooked with onion in butter, stuffed eggs, hot asparagus with lemon-butter and paprika; olives, celery, small bread-and-butter sand-

wiches, camembert cheese and crackers and honey."

INCIDENTALLY, IF YOU want to save yourself a lot of bother and the unpleasantness of standing over boiling hot water washing dishes when it's nearly boiling outside, use paper plates! They have new, gaily decorated grill plates that are a joy.

"I have to be careful not to lose weight when it's so hot," Jean went on. "A number of people do. The best means I've found of preventing that is to drink ovaltine three times a day. But if you want to reduce take lemon juice in cold water without sugar, at least three times daily. It's cooling and slenderizing. Skimmed buttermilk is another very healthy drink. If you want to reduce, the fat particles have to be strained out of it and it's just as beneficial that way.

"And speaking of good drinks, have you ever tried icy-cold pineapple juice—you can get it in cans—as a pick-me-up on a sizzling day? Just keep that in your icebox and the family will be healthy and happy! You can combine it with other juices, too, to make tempting mixtures. For instance, use the pineapple juice with that of lemons, oranges, and strawberries. Chill and sweeten it. Then put in some crushed mint—and you have one of the most refreshing drinks on the market!

"The worst thing people do, though, is to continually chill their system with too many iced foods in summer. Have a warm dish, especially with your dinner. A plate of hot vegetable soup or potassium broth may be a bit warming at the time but they do you good."

These are the two summer dinner menus that Jean has most frequently: Lamb chops, fresh vegetable plate, fruit salad with a dressing of oil, honey and lemon juice, prune whip and lemonade. Chicken, baked potato with skin, spinach, string beans, raw carrot salad, and a fresh fruit cup.

Don't let the summer deaden you. Arrange your diet so that it will give you new life! That's the advice of the lovely Jean Harlow!

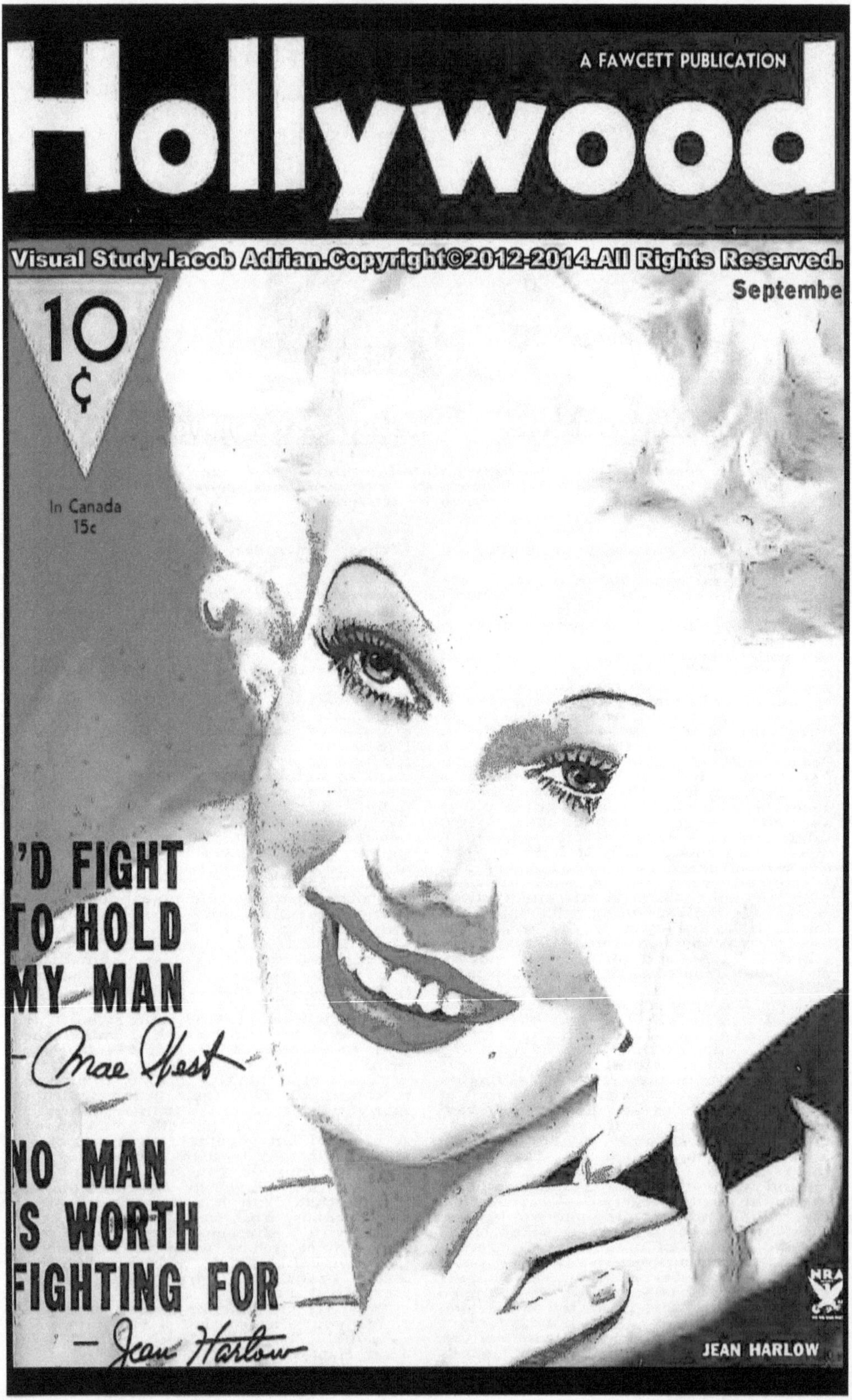

A FAWCETT PUBLICATION

Hollywood

Septembe

10 ¢

In Canada
15¢

'D FIGHT
TO HOLD
MY MAN

— Mae West

NO MAN
IS WORTH
FIGHTING FOR

— Jean Harlow

JEAN HARLOW

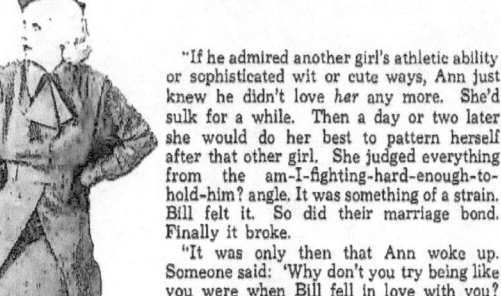

"If he's not worth fighting for he's not worth having!"—Mae West

"If you have to struggle to hold a man's affection he isn't worth the effort!"—Jean Harlow

No man is worth fighting for! —Jean Harlow

question of vital interest to every girl

"You're defeating your own purpose when you think you have to fight to hold your man," says Jean Harlow, who is shown here with Franchot Tone

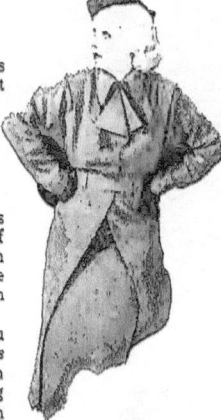

"IF YOU HAVE to struggle to hold a man's affection he isn't worth the effort!" That is how Jean Harlow summarizes it. Jean, who typifies all the freedom and independence of the new era. Who is as modern as tomorrow—and just as unpredictable.

Jean, at twenty-two, has been married three times. Mae West, at thirty-two, has never been married. Both are the kind of women men can't forget. Sensational screen sirens. Glamour girls who know all the answers—but they differ on this one. Listen to what Jean says:

"You're defeating your own end when you so much as think, *I have to fight to hold this man*. You're placing a terrific handicap on your romance. Because you are implying *doubt*. Doubt in your husband, doubt in yourself. No love can live under such conditions. If you enter into marriage with the idea that it's going to be an endurance contest and all other women are your opponents —well, you might as well say 'Good morning, judge!' right then and there.

"I know a girl who had that thought. Just before the wedding bells chimed a wiseacre aunt whispered to her, 'Now, Ann, my dear, *remember* Bill is your particular property. Don't let him out of your grasp for a minute.' And Ann didn't. If Bill came home tired and kissed her a little abstractedly it was a sure sign to her way of thinking that she was slipping in her looks. So she'd go out and get a new dress and an expensive facial.

"I know I fight to hold my men on the screen," Jean Harlow says, "but you're placing too great a handicap on romance when you do this in real life"

"If he admired another girl's athletic ability or sophisticated wit or cute ways, Ann just knew he didn't love *her* any more. She'd sulk for a while. Then a day or two later she would do her best to pattern herself after that other girl. She judged everything from the am-I-fighting-hard-enough-to-hold-him? angle. It was something of a strain. Bill felt it. So did their marriage bond. Finally it broke.

"It was only then that Ann woke up. Someone said: 'Why don't you try being like you were when Bill fell in love with you? Don't work so hard at trying to fascinate him.' It was the soundest advice in the world. They're remarried now. And happy.

● "Why should a woman be different after marriage anyway? Why shouldn't she go right on being a man's sweetheart and treating him like she did when they were engaged? There's no need to take that terribly possessive air with him. He's a free individual. So are you. It's the worst mistake a woman can make to attempt to change herself into something she's not—or to attempt transforming her husband!

"A man falls in love with you because you have certain qualities. Don't alter them after the last of the rice has been thrown. Accentuate them. Do your utmost to make the type you are outstanding. To be definitely, clearly *yourself*. Your best self. Then if you fail, you can't have any regrets." Jean shrugged. There

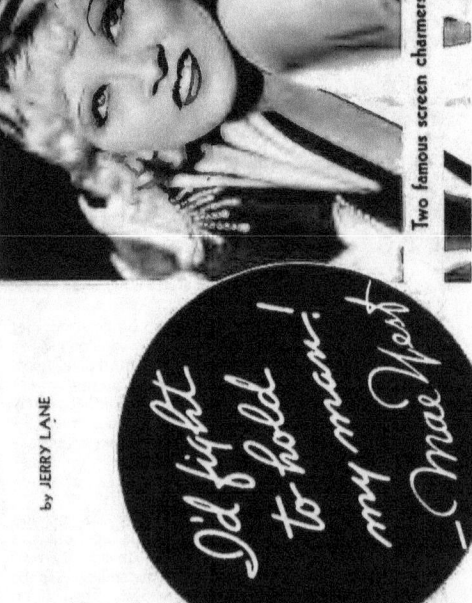

"If he's not worth fighting for he's not worth having!"—Mae West

"If you have to struggle to hold a man's affection he isn't worth the effort!"—Jean Harlow

No man is worth fighting for! —Jean Harlow

I'd fight to hold my man! —Mae West

by JERRY LANE

Two famous screen charmers answer a question of vital interest to every girl

"Any woman can get any man these days. But she's got to be good to keep him." says Mae West

"You're defending your own purpose when you think you have to fight to hold your man," says Jean Harlow, who is shown here with Franchot Tone

Mae West and John Mack Brown in a scene from Lady, *in which she practices the wiles she recommends for real life.*

"I know I fight to hold my man," says Jean Harlow ... "we're planting too great a handicap on this to real life."

"IT's Not Worth fighting for, he's not worth having!" Mae West put plenty of punch behind that statement. The West eyes blazed with the light of battle. Her whole being, baby. It isn't so sin' to wage a good stiff war to keep your man. There were more than 20,000 divorces last year in this country. And if half of those wives hadn't been weak-kneed they wouldn't have been widows now!

Any woman can get any man these days. But a woman can't be good to keep several hundred hot-cha degrees!

"You see, went on Mae, warning up to her subject as only she can, "every man seems always at least potentially in circulation. That's his nature. If you've got an interest to face daily competition from rivals partners. There are plenty of sweet young things ready to get an unhappy man adrift. So—anchor him! Here's the way of it—

"If a girl finds she's losing hold on her man and you've possibly live without she shouldn't waste time sympathizing with herself. Or wondering what's the matter with the man. Or trying to argue him into behaving himself.

"Just let her ask herself: What's the matter with me? Why don't he love me as much as he used to? What have I done? What haven't I done?

"If the girl is frank, she might find that she has fallen into the habit of treating the man like just another common possession. Perhaps she is not making herself as attractive to him physically and mentally as she did when they lighted the torch. Maybe she's forgotten to be the playmate as well as the wife. You can't be a man! You've got to understand his moods and know how to handle him when his moods are upon him. When he wants affection give it to him. When he doesn't, don't try to force it on the poor fellow. Anticipate his likes and dislikes so that you are continually supplying him with pleasant surprises. Keep stepping him up, and deal like kids. When he expects a scolding, give him smiles.

"In short, try to make yourself so completely desirable, so utterly necessary to his well-being and fit into his life so charmingly than he'd rather go out and cut his throat than lose you.

"That all sounds like a pretty tough job, doesn't it? It is. But that is what fighting to hold your man consists of."

● Of course Mae wants it distinctly understood that she doesn't mean for a woman to bury her own personality and be entirely overcome by the man. On the contrary, the more she keeps her individual charm the more he's apt to respect her. She has studied it out in many a drama of the sexes. A large

---

"IT Your Have to struggle to hold a man's affection he isn't worth the effort!" That is how Jean Harlow summarizes it. Jean, to the complete freedom and independence of the new day, is as modern as tomorrow—and just as unpredictable.

Jean, at twenty-two, has been married three times. Mae West, at thirty-two, has never been married. Both are the kind of women you don't forget. Both have been sirens. Glamour girls who know all the answers—but they differ on this one. Listen to what Jean says:

"You're defending your own and when you so much as think, I have to fight to hold this man. You're placing a terrific handicap on your romance. Doubt, in your husband, doubt in yourself. No love can live under such conditions. If you enter into marriage with the idea that it's going to be an endurance contest and all other women are your opponents and that you've got to—your 'Good morning, judge;' right then and there.

"I know a girl who had just thought. Just before the wedding bells chimed a winsome aunt whispered to her. Now, Ann, my dear, remember Bill is your particular property. Don't let him out of your grasp for a minute.' And Ann didn't. If Bill came in half an hour late she immediately flew in her looks. So she'd go out and get a new dress and an expensive facial.

"If he admired another girl's athletic ability or sophisticated wit or cute ways, Ann just knew he didn't love her any more. She'd sulk for a while. Then a day or two later she would do her best to pattern herself from the new—judged everything from the one judged everything hold—him? sink. It was something of a strain Bill felt it. So did their marriage bow Finally it broke.

"It was only then that Ann woke up someone said: 'Why don't you try being like you were when he fell in love with you? Don't work so hard to hold him. Try to hold him.' It was the soundest advice in the world. They're remarried now. And happy.

● "Why should a woman be different after marriage anyway? Why shouldn't she go right on being that sweet heart and treating him like she did sweetheart and treating engaged? There's no need to take that terribly possessive air with him. He's a free individual. So are you. It's the worst mistake a woman can make to attempt to change a wife into something she's not—or to attempt transforming herself.

"A man falls in love with you because you see certain qualities. Don't alter them after the first of the rice has been thrown. Accentuate them. Do your utmost to make the type you are outstanding. To be definitely, clearly yourself. Your best self. Then if you fail, you can't have any regrets." Jean shrugged. There

An Open Letter to JEAN HARLOW

from J. EUGENE CHRISMAN

DEAR JEAN:
To the outside world, which knows you only for your screen characterizations, you may be just Jean Harlow, platinum-blonde *Circe*, exponent of Sex Appeal. It may consider you a favorite of whatever gods there be, living a private life of silken luxury, without a care in the world. But I know the real Jean Harlow, the gallant lady who, when life attempts to beat her down, faces the battle, unafraid. I know her for one of the most genuine, most charming and most regular of people. That is the girl I want to talk about.

I am happy to be called your friend, Jean. I do not think you give your confidence or your friendship lightly. Once it is given, it is something to be prized and cherished. The world out-side may believe you as light and as fickle as some of your screen rôles would indicate but Hollywood knows you as a fine friend, a brave fighter, a splendid pal.

● I have followed your career ever since you were cast in *Hell's Angels* but we did not meet until you were making *Red Headed Woman*. It was the day you played the bedroom scene, remember, and you were nursing a swollen jaw where Chester Morris had socked you. It was all for the sake of realism but it hurt. You took it without a whimper, just as you have taken every blow that life ever dealt you. After that we met many times. You were kind enough to have me at your home. We met on sets where you were working. Then one day, while you were making *The Girl from Missouri*, we sat in your car outside the sound stage and just talked, a friendly chat. Then, for the first time, I felt that I knew the real Jean Harlow.

There are so many things about which I could write you but since this letter is to be read by millions who are your fans, I think I would

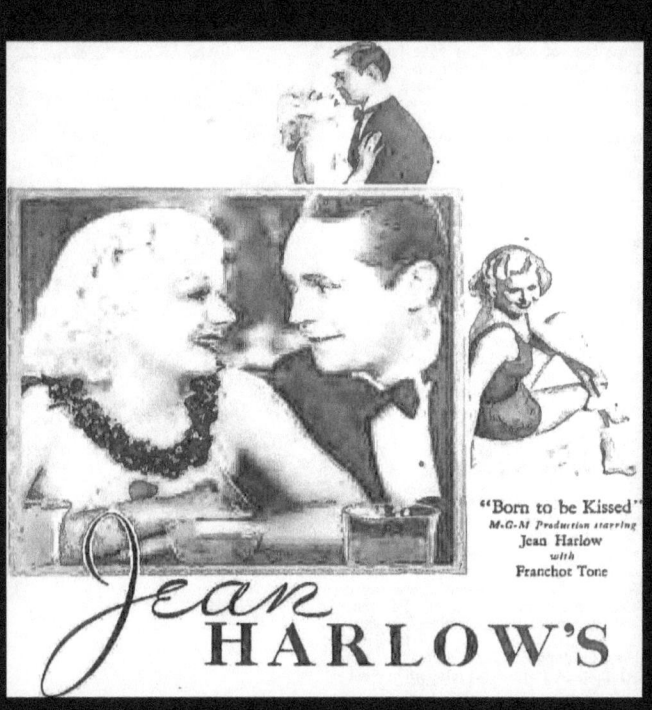

"Born to be Kissed"
M-G-M Production starring
Jean Harlow
with
Franchot Tone

Jean HARLOW'S

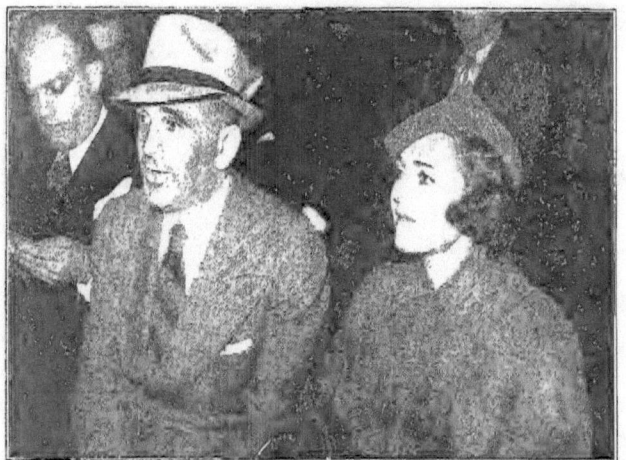

Ruby Keeler and Al Jolson like fights, but they go to the ring to see them, for Ruby and Al are one of Hollywood's most happily married couples. Here they are at the Hollywood Legion Stadium

An Open Letter to Jean Harlow

like them to know how you think of them. I want them to know with what respect you regard those people whose loyalty and allegiance have put you where you are today, at the top of the ladder of cinema fame. More, perhaps, than any other star of the screen, you are loyal to your fans.

Too many cinema celebrities, once they reach the top, are prone to forget that it was the nickels and dimes of their admirers, thrust through the boxoffice windows, which made them. They begin to think that it was their own unaided efforts which brought them to the top. But not you, Jean! I have noticed that one of your favorite topics is appreciation of your fans. Your fan mail is the highest of any Metro star and yet not a single letter, no matter how unimportant, is unanswered. I happen to know that you employ three people, full time, to assist you in seeing that not a single admirer goes without a personal reply.

THE REFRESHING thing about you, Jean, is that you enjoy being a movie star and admit it. You are not annoyed when autograph hunters accost you and demand that you write in their books. You once said to me:

"After all I'm only human. Sometimes when I am a wreck, completely exhausted from long hours in the studio, it is almost a temptation to run when people crowd around me. But I always pull myself together and smile for them. After all, they are my fans and it's to them that I owe everything that I am today."

Once we sat in that great white living room of yours and you told me something of what the world-wide admiration of your fans has done for you. You told me, in all sincerity, that such adoration would prevent anyone from being a cynic. You told me of how the letters which come to you, share every turn of your fortunes, your happiness and your sorrow, your triumphs and your disappointments. When the bad breaks came and when the skies were gray, you told me how touched you were when thousands of loving fans came to your aid with their letters of encouragement and confidence in you.

You told me also of something else these fans of yours have done for you. They have made you live up to their ideals of you. They have forced you to improve your mind, to read good books, to study, so that you might be their intellectual ideal. Their pride in your personal self caused you to watch your diet, and exercise to keep your body slender for them. They caused you to take even more than a normal pride in your clothes, so that when you appeared in public, you were the Jean Harlow of their dreams and their ideals.

MORE THAN 15,000 fan letters pour in on you every week. Thousands only desire to express their admiration and their loyalty. Others make requests for help. Even if you had the wealth of a Midas you could not help all those who make appeals but it isn't because you are unaware of their need. It is simply because you cannot respond.

But it hasn't all been a bed of roses, Jean. How well I know that. I have seen you smile beneath the agony of a sudden thrust which life has made at you. But I do not believe, Jean, that life can ever get you down.

Then too, another beautiful thing in your life is your love for your mother. She is a charming person, whose entire life is wrapped up in her *Baby*. She once told me that she had put me on her white list, because I had been nice to *Baby*. The old saying that a girl's best friend is her mother, is no misquotation in your case, Jean.

THE ONLY thing that worries the folks who worship you, Jean, is your seeming inability to find married happiness.

Three marriages have turned out wrong for you, all, I happen to know, through no fault of your own. It seems to me, Jean, that the one thing you need to make your life complete, is the love of a fine man. I think if your fans could know that you had found the one man on earth who could make you completely happy, there would be rejoicing all over the world.

I am glad to see that you like the company of William (Bill) Powell. He is also a friend of mine. I can understand so easily, knowing you both as I do, why you seek each other's company. Bill, unless I am mistaken, is the best prescription for you that the doctor could order. That keen mind of his, that stimulating sense of humor, that charm and polish which hides the soul of an urchin, is just what you need. Perhaps it's only friendship and not romance, Jean, I don't know, but I do know it's what you have needed for a long time.

Bravo Jean and *au revoir*. What this country needs is not a good five-cent cigar but more Jean Harlows. I hope, when you answer this, that you'll give your fans a glance at the real Jean, the one I know. I'll be seeing you and don't forget, we haven't yet found time to play that game of golf.

Always your friend,

J. Eugene Chrisman

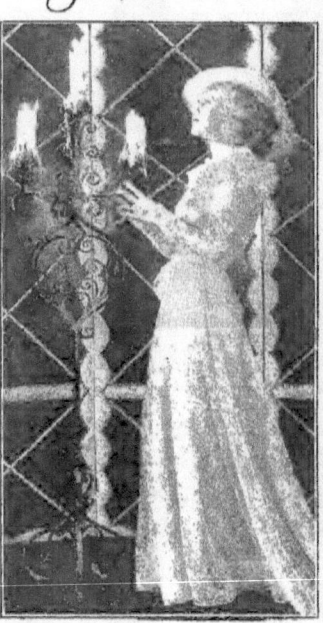

Youthful simplicity marked the lovely wedding gown worn by Ginger Rogers when she became the bride of Lew Ayres. It is fashioned of Aquamarine Chantilly lace

Jean Harlow Replies to

J. EUGENE CHRISMAN

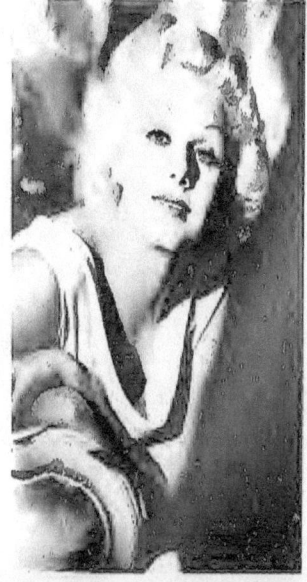

DEAR GENE:
Your open letter to me in last month's HOLLYWOOD was one of the most gracious gestures I have known. It is needless to say that I thank you sincerely.

You mention my feeling of loyalty to the people who, as you so adequately phrased it, are the real reason for whatever success that I may have today. I believe, Gene, that you know what friendship means to me. It is one of the motivating factors of my life. These people have more than proved their friendship for me.

I feel that you have given me too much credit for the manner in which, as you expressed it in your letter, I have "taken it on the chin." When it is a case of sink or swim, you usually swim. I have tried to live up to the ideas and ideals that have been instilled in me from childhood, which includes sportsmanship.

We all know that in everyone's life there are bitter disappointments. If we were to allow ourselves to be warped by these experiences, or to allow them to make us bitter or cynical, then we would not deserve the compensations that life always offers for those things.

Somehow, to me, life has always been like going through grammar school, high school and college. In each class we have problems of one sort or another to solve, and when we have solved them satisfactorily, we are then ready to go on to a higher class and learn more. The most valuable lessons we learn in this life, to my way of thinking, are tolerance, gratitude and the real meaning and application of that misused Golden Rule: "Do unto others as you would have them do unto you."

Regarding your reference to my mother, my only reply to that is that I am certainly one of the most fortunate persons in this funny old world of ours to have as a parent a person with such sound and fine fundamental principles, such a divine sense of humor and such an unselfish love for her family.

Gene, you mentioned the fact that I enjoy being a movie star. I do. I enjoy the things the position offers, such as intensely interesting work, the charming and talented people with whom I work, and the true joy of having a job that MUST be done. Also, the sense of personal satisfaction (this in no way has anything to do with ego) that a job finished, to the best of one's ability, gives.

As to my friend, Mr. Powell—again I feel that I am more than fortunate. If you can find as many laughs in a week with twenty people as you can in half an hour with Bill Powell, I still haven't met the people or found the week.

Bill and I haven't found time to become romantic about each other, and I'm afraid we never will find the time. His friendship has been a great mental stimulus to me, as well as a stimulus to my sense of humor. A more clear-thinking, intelligent, fair-minded individual, you could never find.

Speaking of that long-promised game of golf, how about bringing along a pal? Bill loves to play and many of our happy hours together have been on the golf course. Only let me warn you—bring some sandwiches. Because we very often arrive at about the fifth hole and get into an intense argument and we simply take time out for awhile.

And now, Gene, I just must say a word to you. I treasure your friendship for me and your friendliness toward me more than I can say.

With deep affection,

Jean Harlow

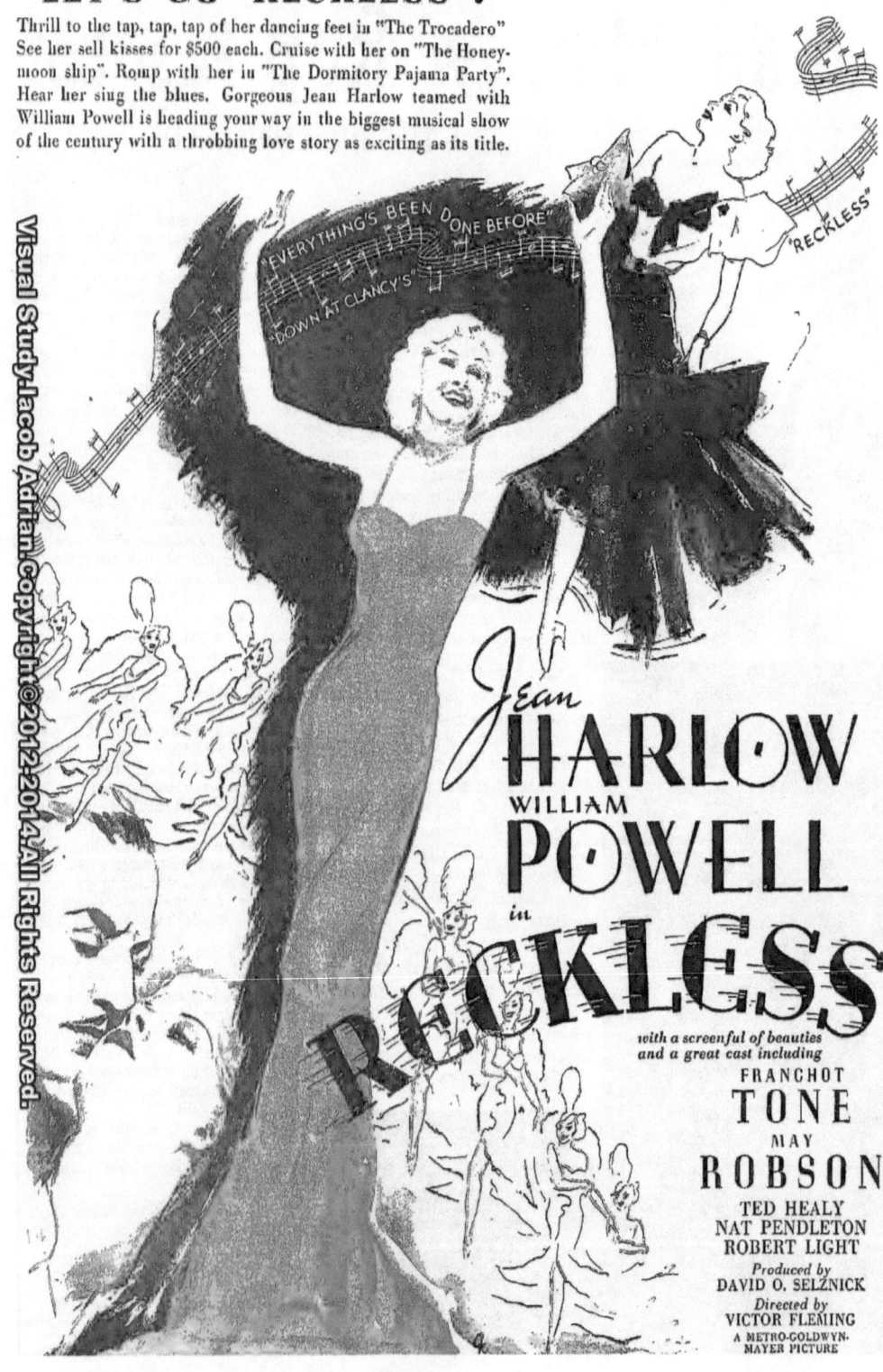

LET'S GO "RECKLESS"!

Thrill to the tap, tap, tap of her dancing feet in "The Trocadero"
See her sell kisses for $500 each. Cruise with her on "The Honey-
moon ship". Romp with her in "The Dormitory Pajama Party".
Hear her sing the blues. Gorgeous Jean Harlow teamed with
William Powell is heading your way in the biggest musical show
of the century with a throbbing love story as exciting as its title.

"EVERYTHING'S BEEN DONE BEFORE"

"DOWN AT CLANCY'S"

"RECKLESS"

JEAN
HARLOW
WILLIAM
POWELL
in
RECKLESS

with a screenful of beauties
and a great cast including

FRANCHOT
TONE

MAY
ROBSON

TED HEALY
NAT PENDLETON
ROBERT LIGHT

Produced by
DAVID O. SELZNICK
Directed by
VICTOR FLEMING
A METRO-GOLDWYN-
MAYER PICTURE

What I Think

JEAN HARLOW

by

Clark Gable

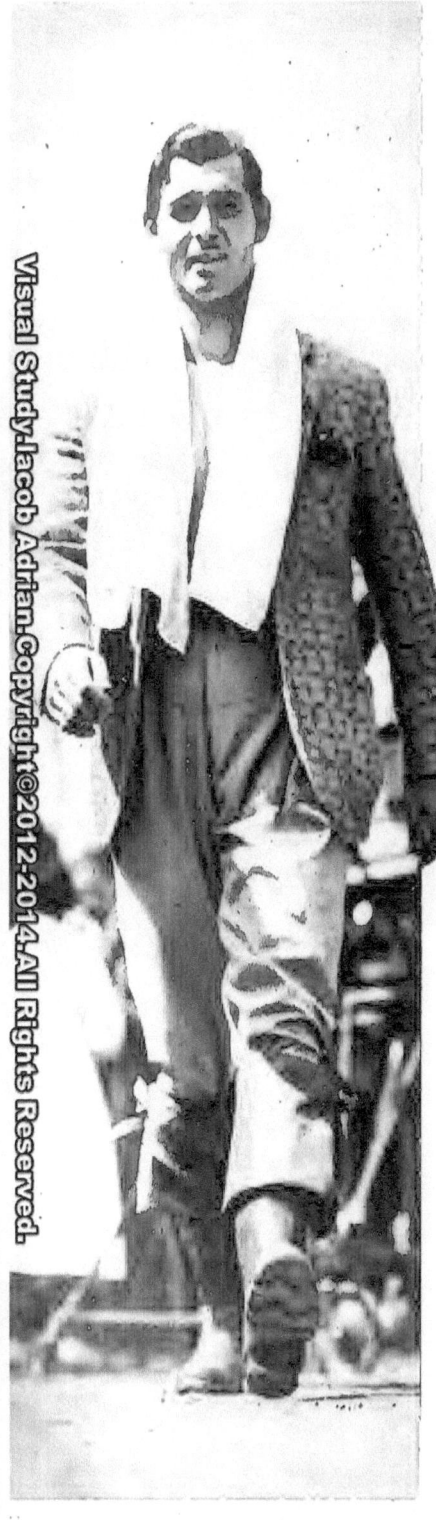

To Me, Jean always seems to have rather a man's attitude toward life. I don't know just how to explain this, but I always feel it when I'm with her. You can talk to her so naturally. She understands and appreciates the things men are interested in. Of course this appeals to any man.

Instead of the slinky evening gowns and bizarre costumes you might expect her to wear, after seeing her on the screen, she usually goes around in a pair of slacks, or a sports skirt, short socks, and sneakers. She seems utterly unconscious of her beauty.

She adores golf. She is an expert fisherman. She loves riding. And she makes no allowances for herself as a woman in these sports. She plays them on an equal basis with men—and discusses them more intelligently than one woman in a hundred.

She never uses her femininity in conversations—to win arguments, for instance, or to put over a point. So many women suddenly "go feminine" when they think it will turn the tide their way, but I don't think Jean even thinks of her sex in such circumstances.

● She Has, Too, a complete sense of fairness. I don't know anyone, man or woman, who is more of a straight shooter. She is fair in the things she does and the things she says. I have seen her, on one occasion, give a bit player an unusual break. The girl had a short line to speak, and then Jean was supposed to interrupt her. The girl had tried awfully hard, but as the scene was to be played she would be hardly noticed. Jean said, "I was an extra myself once, so I know what this means to her. Couldn't we change the script a little so my line can be delayed—and so I won't have to walk in front of her?"

I've never known Jean to "go temperamental," and when you consider the number of days we have worked together, this is a real tribute. I have seldom seen her out of spirits. Of course, she's human, and she has occasional flare-ups. But they last only a short time and are always directed where they belong. Usually she is right.

She's a swell sport. For instance, if I have to "sock" her in a picture—and believe me, it is done with the utmost reluctance!—she never asks me to take it easy. She doesn't expect me to. When I "dunked" her in the barrel of water in "*Red Dust*," she didn't seem to mind at all. I'm always a bit embarrassed about such scenes, and her attitude helps. It's just part of the business to her, and she goes through the retakes, if they're necessary, like a trouper.

Again, during the making of *China Seas*, she had a bad cold, and right in the middle of it we had

Two Pals

other,

Mark

About
CLARK GABLE
by
Jean Harlow

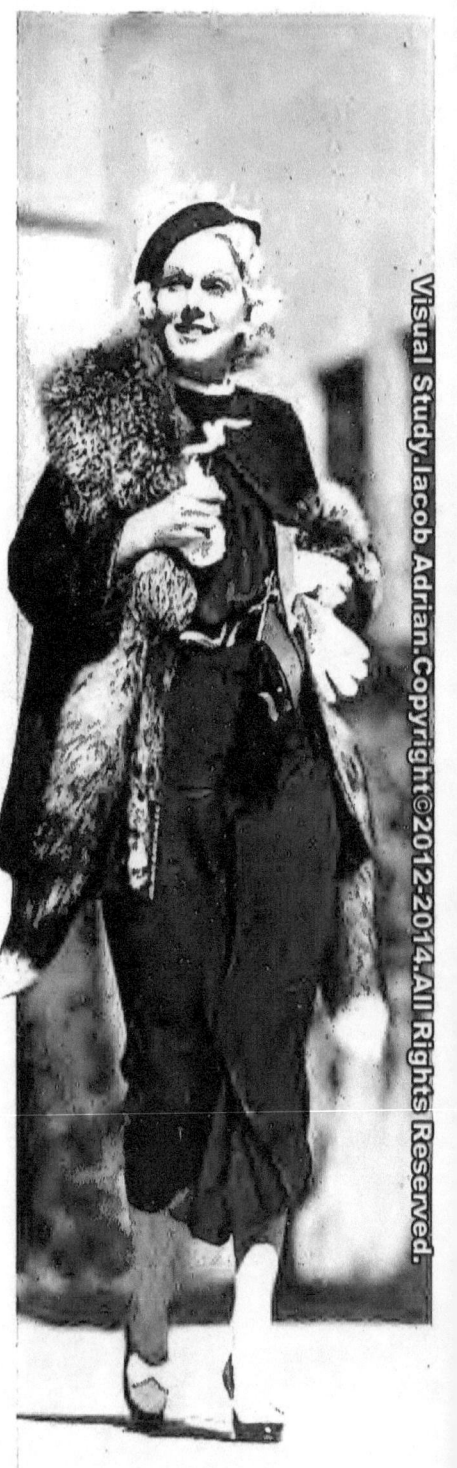

I CAN'T IMAGINE anyone I'd rather have for a friend than Clark Gable. He embodies all the qualities which are necessary for true friendship.

Not more than half a dozen people in Hollywood, I believe, know Clark as he really is. He is so much deeper than people think. He won't talk about himself—he doesn't even seem to *think* much about himself. It's not that he's a Garbo. But he is always so interested in finding out about you that he never tells you much about Gable.

But I know him from the standpoint of one who has worked with him on many pictures. I believe that by working with a man you get to know him as well as anyone possibly can. If he stands well in the opinion of his fellow-workers, he'll be the same under any conditions.

We started our screen partnership several years ago in *The Secret Six*. It was my first picture after *Hell's Angels* and it was, I think, Clark's first important picture. Since then we have played together in *Red Dust*, *Hold Your Man*, and now in *China Seas*. The most revealing comment I can make about Clark is that he is, today, the same human, natural, amusing chap he was in the beginning.

He has made a spectacular success. His rise to the top is breath-taking even in Hollywood, where overnight fame comes fairly often. He is probably every woman's ideal of a man, as a husband, friend, or a lover. But Clark is no more conscious of this than he is conscious of the color of his eyes. Maybe even less so! Fame hasn't changed him.

expose each
as told to
Dowling

For instance, his stand-in now is a man who worked with him on the stage some ten years ago. Clark's attitude toward this chap is that of a friend and a fellow-worker. He doesn't seem to have a trace of a feeling that would be, after all, quite natural in the circumstances—"I'm the star and you're the stand-in!"

There's one exception, one change that has come inevitably with success. When Clark and I made *The Secret Six* we had no particular incentive because it seemed too wildly improbable that we would become stars. We regarded each bit of success as a lucky "break" and made the most of it. Our attitude was happy-go-lucky. We enjoyed ourselves as we went along.

Now Clark regards his work with an increased seriousness. He takes each part more intensely. The best way of putting it is to say that he has an *increased application* to his rôles.

● HE IS ESSENTIALLY a man's man. His attitude toward me is that of a pal or a brother. With some men, you are made awfully conscious of being a woman.

What I Think About Jean Harlow

another scene where she had to be soaked. She didn't complain once, though I'm sure it was anything but pleasant for her. And if she didn't have such radiant health, it would take her weeks to break up the resulting cold.

One of the characteristics I have in mind when I say she has a man's attitude is her amazing sincerity. She is always perfectly frank. There is no halfway about her, she treats everyone the same way,—director, producer, or fellow-actor. When we were making *The Secret Six*, Wallace Beery once criticised her for some minor detail of her performance. Without hesitation she flared right back at him. Remember, at the time, her position wasn't nearly so important as his. But he admired her frankness—I believe their friendship dates from that day.

She never keeps things pent up inside herself. She doesn't nourish a grudge. If she has anything to say, she brings it out into the open, and then forgets about it. I like that.

❂ LOOKING BACK on our first picture together, the talks we had will always stand out in my mind. After her success in *Hell's Angels,* she was a step ahead of me on the way to success, yet she never made me feel that it was her picture any more than mine.

Neither of us knew much about the business, and we tried to figure things out together so the rest wouldn't realize how awfully green we really were. I remember Jean would ask me at the end of every scene—"How'm I doing?"

And I asked her the same.

We criticised each other, trying desperately to learn. Nobody else seemed to pay much attention to us. We were not among the chosen few who saw the daily rushes. Every good word Jean heard about me, she would rush to repeat to me. And things that weren't so good, too, because she knew that is one way of progressing.

We used to plan, jokingly, what we wanted if we ever did get to the top. Jean never particularly wanted fame. The lights and the crowds and the glamour of being a star never seemed to mean much to her, even before she had them. She wanted, sincerely, the happiness of knowing she had done a job well.

If you talked to her directors and other fellow-stars, I think you'll find that she feels the same way today.

She was, I remember, terribly afraid of being typed in "vamp" rôles. She was afraid that her part in *Hell's Angels* would mark her forever in the eyes of the fans. *Red Dust* wasn't much better. But she didn't complain.

She is, in my opinion, one of Hollywood's best comédiennes, and I feel that she is right in wanting to do more comedy. Certainly few stars in Hollywood could have equalled her wonderful performance in *Bombshell*. I hope she is given the chance to do more pictures like that.

She is a thoughtful person, considerate of those around her. Every morning she has coffee and doughnuts on the set. Instead of ordering one cup of coffee and a couple of doughnuts sent to her dressing room, she orders a huge pot of coffee and a couple of dozen doughnuts for the entire company.

Because of little things like this, every extra I've ever talked with adores her. Sometimes they are critical of other stars, who may be, in their eyes, ritzy or up-stage. But Jean stands ace high with all of them.

Having grown out of the extra ranks herself, she has not forgotten her friends and acquaintances among them. Out of every crowd, on our pictures, she will find a familiar face or two. It's always—"Hello, Eddie!"—"Hi, there, Janet!"

❂ SHE HAS boundless enthusiasm—a quality so many people outgrow. In many ways she is like a kid in her pleasure over little things. Just the other day a property boy who had worked with her on *Bombshell* brought her a live rabbit. She couldn't have been more pleased if it had been an expensive gift.

Because they like her, everyone who works with her tries to make things easier for her—even though she isn't a demanding person, and prefers to do things for herself. She has told me of making the dance scene in *Reckless*. She had never danced for the camera and was terribly nervous. She had to do her stuff in front of a hundred or so bit players—all of them chosen for their expert dancing. If they had so much as whispered a word of criticism, she told me, she wouldn't have been able to go through with it. Instead they applauded her, and kept crying out, "That's the stuff, Jean!"—"You've got it now!"

And their enthusiasm meant so much to her that by the third "take" she was dancing like a professional!

It has always been a bond between us that we started at about the same time, and our progress has been more or less parallel. Neither of us can remember "way back to the silent days." We went to the same class in the same school, in other words, and we've been promoted in the same pictures. Of course, in between, we each went separate ways, she with other leading men and I with other leading ladies.

After a picture, we make no effort to keep up our friendship. But when we see each other again, we seem to pick up where we left off, regardless of what has happened to us in the meantime. It's marvellous and rare to have a friend like that. Most friendships are lost unless they are kept alive.

Probably this outburst puts me in the class of her fans. I am. And I think you'll find that everyone who really knows Jean feels just the same way.

A CHALLENGE TO ALL SCREEN HISTORY!

Think back to your greatest film thrill! Recall the mightiest moments of romance, action, soul=adventure of the screen! A picture has come to top them all! For many months Hollywood has marvelled at the stu= pendous production activities at the M=G=M studios, not equalled since "Ben Hur"; for many months three great film stars and a brilliant cast have enacted the elemental drama of this primitive love story. Deeply etched in your memory will be Clark Gable as the handsome seafar= ing man; Jean Harlow as the frank beauty of Oriental ports; Wallace Beery as the bluff trader who also seeks her affections. "China Seas" is the first attraction with which M=G=M starts its new Fall entertain= ment season. We predict its fame will ring lustily down the years to come!

CLARK

GABLE

JEAN

HARLOW

WALLACE

BEERY

CHINA SEAS

with

Lewis STONE · Rosalind RUSSELL

Directed by Tay Garnett · Associate Producer: Albert Lewin

A METRO=GOLDWYN= 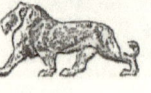 MAYER PICTURE

JEAN HARLOW'S
Code of Living

Everything in life has a price tag, says Jean. If you are a good bargain hunter, you will pay the price and never regret it. Otherwise—!

by MARK DOWLING

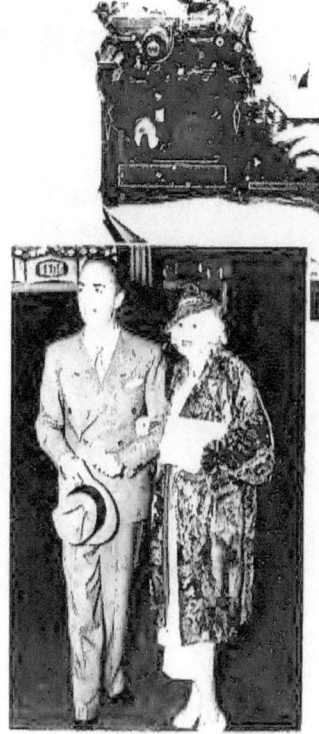

Behind Jean's tantalizing allure is the fine, honest mind of a man . . . Here is a man's code of living, and a man's way of thinking

JEAN HARLOW told me, "Friendship is more important to me than romance. I'd rather have a man for a lifelong friend than have him make romantic love to me for an evening. And perhaps because I do not expect romance, I haven't had very much of it in my life. I could count on the fingers of one hand the men who have spent an evening making love to me. We get to laughing over an amusing joke. We discuss a serious topic that is vital to him. The men I know regard me as a friend, on a man to man basis, rather than as a woman who must be paid subtle flattery and pretty compliments. And that's the way I want it."

Perhaps Jean's tremendous sincerity came because love has hurt her and brought tragedy so often into her twenty-four years. She told me once, quietly, "Perhaps I am not meant for marriage. . . ."

More likely, men appreciate beneath her tantalizing body and the platinum beauty which has become a worldwide trademark for allure—the fine, honest mind of a man.

Jean lives by a man's code, with a sense of sportsmanship and fairness that make her rare among women. A man friend of hers told me once:

"It's so much fun to be with her, on a comradeship basis, that you almost forget her feminine attraction. If you do try to make love to her, she puts you off with a laugh or a clever joke. She has, you know, a brilliant sense of humor. Instead of love-making, you spend the time laughing with her!

"You can, too, talk over things with Jean that you would hesitate to discuss with other women. She has a fine mind, alert and trained. You feel that she has met many responsibilities in her life, and faced them bravely."

● JEAN SAYS herself, "Marino Bello, my step-father, comes to me with his business problems just as he would to a son instead of a daughter. I don't

Jean is seen constantly with William Powell these days. This was snapped at the preview of Powell's newest picture, *Escapade*

know why. He would never dream of bothering my mother, for instance, with such things.

"My grandfather, you know, always wanted a grandson instead of a daughter. When I came, he raised me as a boy. He taught me two things I have never forgotten. One was the golden rule. So simple that it sounds deceptively easy to follow, I find that it affects everything I do, every human contact I have. *Do unto others as you would have them do unto you.*

"The other lesson he taught me was that life can be like a great department store. Everything has its price tag. He warned me against paying more than I could afford for any article. But

when the bill came, if it seemed too high, not to complain. After all, *I* bought it.

"These rules in themselves provide a code of living. If you follow them, you can't go wrong. Whatever people say of you, you will always know that you have done nothing to be ashamed of. *You can live with yourself*—that, in life, is the important thing.

"Sportsmanship is another vital point in my code. To be a good winner and a good loser. And if I lose, not to whine about it. No one is interested in my troubles. And the more I think about them and discuss them, the worse they seem. Therefore it's best to take one's losses gallantly. I try to remember that the people I admire most are those who don't weigh me down with their private worries.

"Fairness, too, is terribly important. It sounds easy to say that everyone has a right to his or her opinions. But it isn't always easy to carry out. I don't believe in criticising people. After all, who am I to judge? And sometimes I know the act, but not the motive behind it, which is all important. I can remember an unjust criticism that was made of me. Later, the person came to apologize. How much easier to have tried, at first, to understand my motive in what I had done!"

● A WOMAN FRIEND who has long been closely associated with Jean told me, "I have never heard her gossip or

Jean Harlow's Code of Living

repeat gossip about anyone. If she joins a group who are indulging in catty remarks about this star or that producer, she doesn't even seem interested. She never repeats rumors or whispered talk. When you consider what a hot-bed of gossip Hollywood is, that's a record."

There are other examples of her man's attitude. Clark Gable told me that she never uses her feminine appeal to win arguments, or to gain her ends, and she speaks from the stand-point of a fellow-star who has appeared in several important pictures with her. Another associate of Jean's at the studio told me, "She has never once been late for an appointment, even though tardiness is supposed to be a beautiful woman's r i g h t . She never breaks a date, or offers excuses."

Jean says simply, "I expect that much consideration from others, and it's part of my code of living not to ask more than I am willing to give."

● FRANKNESS Is one of her chief characteristics. At the studio her fellow-workers admire her for her frankness in speaking up whenever she feels things aren't going right. She never nurses a grudge or cherishes a grievance. A director with whom she once openly disagreed is now one of her close friends.

She has a personal disregard of lovely clothes. At the studio, for pictures, she drapes her beautiful body in creations designed to bring out every bit of her appeal. At home, when she is not working, she wears a pair of white sneakers, and a sports dress. And looks, incidentally, as ravishing as if she wore the latest Adrian gown.

Radiantly healthy, she adores the outdoor sports of men and plays them without a woman's handicap. She excels at tennis and riding and golf. She loves to swim in the crystal water of her swimming pool. She goes for long drives alone in her car, as carefree as a man of the wind whipping her platinum locks.

Still, tantalizing, she is utterly feminine, even though she scorns to make use of woman's tricks and wiles. She is man-like only in her code of living—her honesty, fairness, and willingness to face trouble if it comes.

"In the last analysis, a man's and a woman's minds are completely different on fundamental topics," Jean told me. Such as love, for instance. I am completely feminine, naturally. Even though I believe that frankness, sometimes considered a man's characteristic rather than a feminine one, is as vital in marriage as it is in business or friendship. Talking things out frankly, I believe, solves more problems than nursing our wounds in secret.

". . . r marriage is not working out to be the ideal thing they had hoped, I think it is best to be straightforward and discuss the trouble openly. Even if the other person may not feel the same way. Then there is a sharp clean wound, and it heals quicker."

If love comes to her again, it will come in the guise of friendship. And romance must come, even though she wards it off with a ready laugh. It could not be otherwise, with her blue eyes, her softly curved lips, and her radiant loveliness.

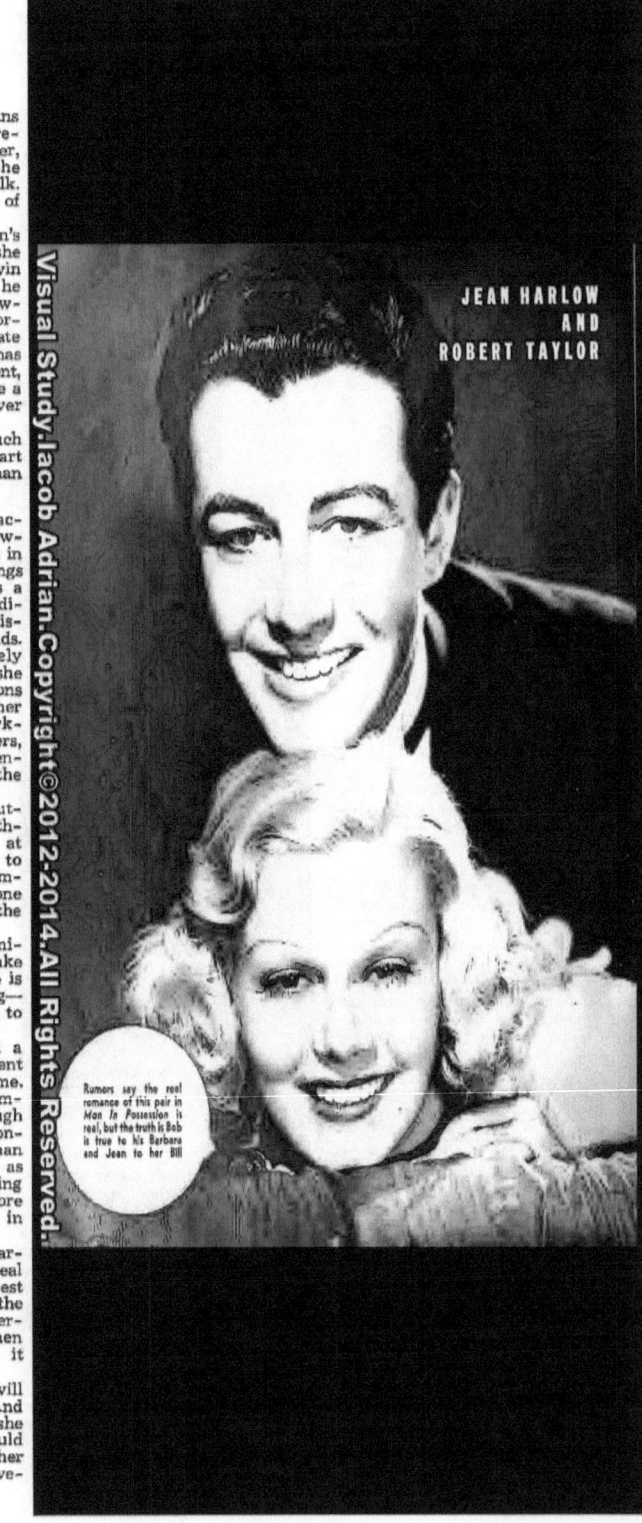

JEAN HARLOW
AND
ROBERT TAYLOR

Rumors say the real romance of this pair in Man In Possession is real, but the truth is Bob is true to his Barbara and Jean to her Bill

MY DAUGHTER

Pals, these two? The very closest!
You'll love this colorful story on
how they've spent the years

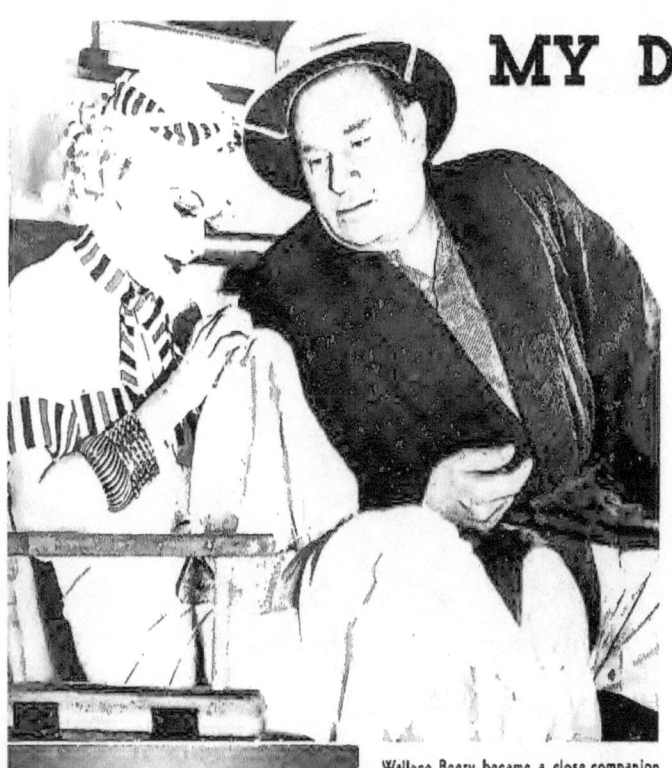

Wallace Beery became a close companion
of Jean's during the filming of *China Seas*.
When they weren't acting, he talked and
she sewed over in a far corner

J EAN IS AN interesting combination
of woman and child. Before she
was born, I determined that I
wouldn't be just a Mother, that I
would also be her best friend. In making that resolution I realized that a
best friend never interferes with the
rights of another person; never adopts
that superior "I know best" attitude;
and I have never taken it with Jean.
With the result that we have, through
all the different stages of her life been,
not only mother and daughter, but the
closest of friends.

When she was tiny and helpless, I
was the usual, doting, adoring mother,
loving every little thing I could do
for her and dreading to even think of
the time when she would be capable
of doing things for herself. I think
the most tearful day of my life was
when she announced that she wanted
to take her bath "aw by mysef." I
felt that my baby was growing away
from me. However, I might have
spared myself those foolish tears for
although the years gave me a lovely,
understanding friend, they did not rob
me entirely of my baby.

● JEAN WAS NEVER a helpless child.
From the time she could sit on
the floor and put her right chubby foot

into her left stubby shoe, she had an
air of independence about her. Still
to this day, she remains very childish
in many ways.

One of her childish habits that she
clings to is that only I must wake her
up in the morning. Her room is sepa-
rated from mine by what she chooses
to call her "health room." This room
contains a massage table, a hair drier,
vitalizer, and other things necessary to
health and beauty. In the morning
the maid brings a glass of hot water
and lemon juice to my room and I take
it with me when I awaken Jean.

She always wakes up smiling. She
drinks the liquid I have brought her
and then hurries into her bath and I
hurry into mine. It's always a little
race to see who will finish first.

Then we both climb into my bed for
breakfast which is served to us on a
tray. As we eat we take pads and
pencils and make our plans for the
day. And I must say for Jean that
she tries to plan her day so that she
can spend as much time as possible
with me.

● SOMETIMES WHEN I LOOK over her
plans for the day I am amazed.
It doesn't seem possible that one girl
could do so many things. Yet she always carries out her plans without
seeming to hurry or wear herself out.
The secret of this is that she never
wastes a moment—every appointment
dovetails with the next, be it work or
play.

From the time Jean first started to
have her own ideas, she has discussed
them with me frankly. To encourage
that trait in her, I have never tried
to force my opinions on her. I give
advice naturally, but the final decision
is and always has been, up to Jean.
If her decision does not turn out for
the best, I do not criticize; I only try
to do everything I can to straighten
matters out.

When Jean is working, her entire
time is given over to her work and
things pertaining to it; such as inter-
views, photographs, wardrobe fittings,
and a dozen and one other things that
picture people must crowd into a day.
She usually takes her luncheon with
her to the studio. Her luncheon consists of something very light but nour-
ishing.

Jean cannot do without sleep. She
must have, at least, nine hours every
night. As soon as she finishes on the

JEAN HARLOW

By Mrs. Marino Bello

(as told to
Harmony Haynes)

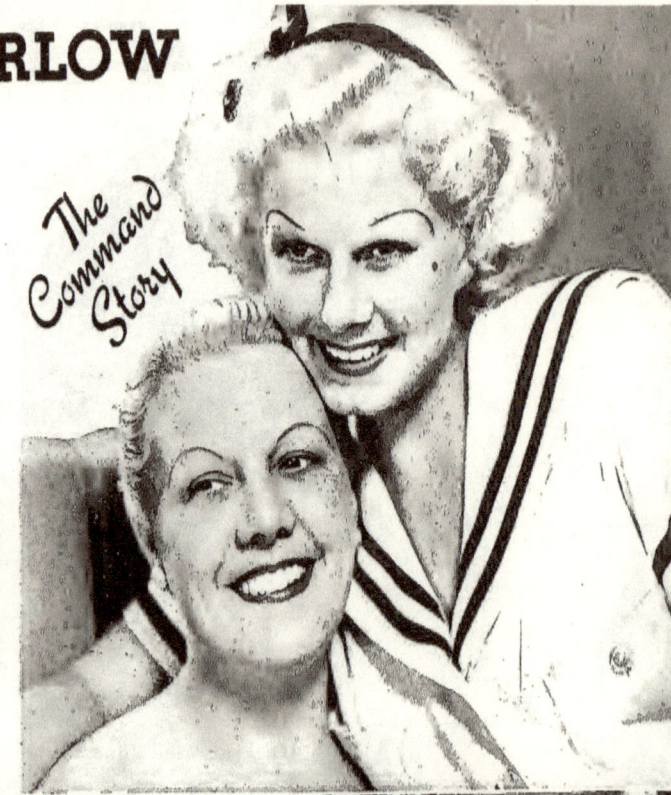

The
Command
Story

set, she goes to her dressing-room, removes her make-up, has her hair fingerwaved; and also has it shampooed, not less than three times a week. Jean is very fastidious; she cannot tolerate anything about her that isn't fresh and clean; and she feels that because her hair is so very light that it soils quickly.

Before she leaves the studio, wardrobe and other things necessary for the next day's work are in readiness so that it is fairly late when she arrives home. She immediately bathes, sometimes she has a massage and sometimes not, but she goes right to bed. She eats a little dinner of cottage cheese, she wouldn't think it was dinner if she didn't have her cottage cheese, three or four green vegetables, and a glass of milk. After dinner she visits a short time with me and then to sleep.

● THE DAYS WHEN she does not work are spent very much as any other young girl might spend them. Swimming, tennis, having friends in to luncheon or tea, or going over her wardrobe. She seldom goes out. She never did care to go out but she does like to have guests come to her home, especially if they drop in informally. I think that is due to the fact that Jean would rather serve than be served. Even when she and I are alone, she will slip into the kitchen and make rolls and serve them to me for luncheon as a little surprise.

Jean is really like a child about surprises. Anything and everything will please her if it is delivered as one. And even greater is her pleasure in surprising others. She loves birthdays or holidays.

For instance on my birthday, Jean always gets up long before I am awake and covers my bed with flowers that she has picked from the garden. Then she awakens me with the song, Happy Birthday to You! The entire day is one surprise after the other until night time when the "real" surprise is delivered. And when her own birthday rolls around she seems to think it is another day in which the honors should be mine. On her last birthday, she presented me with a town car. It always seems as if she were thanking me for having given her life.

● SHE LIKES TO BE surprised herself. I know she would be extremely disappointed if I didn't hide colored

easter eggs all over the house and grounds so she could hunt for them Easter morning. And Christmas! It wouldn't be Christmas, no matter how many lovely gifts she received, if she didn't find her stocking filled with silly little presents.

That is one reason she so loves her fans. They send her so many thoughtful little gifts and cards and letters. One girl recently sent her a little elephant hair ring for good luck and Jean wears it all the time. She never lets a letter go unanswered and never fails to acknowledge receipt of a gift.

Not so long ago she was made an honorary Fire Chief and given a "FIRE" sign and a blue light to put on her car. With it is given the privilege of going faster than the law ordinarily allows. Jean doesn't want to do that and I wouldn't permit the driver to go over thirty-five miles an hour under any circumstances so Jean never makes use of the privilege.

Yet she loves her light and her sign. Shortly after they were presented to her, a policeman stopped the car and thinking she had no right to them, wanted her

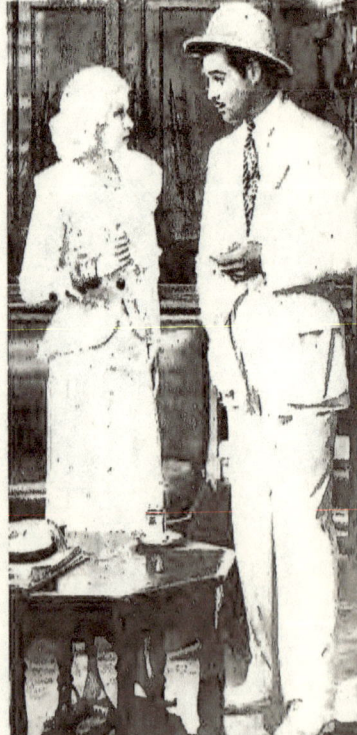

Mother and daughter display many of the same characteristics in the above photo. Below, Jean and Clark Gable doing a scene together in China Seas

My Daughter, Jean Harlow

to give them up. She was afraid he was going to take them from her and she actually cried. She *wanted* her light and her sign. She still has them.

Jean has four pets, a dog, two yellow Persian cats and a white bunny. The cats are twins and look so much alike that she cannot tell them apart so she has never named them. They have first right to any place in the house. Jean calls them every night before she goes to bed and insists that they either sleep in her room or mine and on the best pillow! The bunny was given her by a property boy at the studio as an Easter gift and no one in the house can feed that bunny but Jean herself.

● JEAN Is very thoughtful of other people. As a child, I never had to ask her or tell her to share her toys with other children. So even today with all the things she must do, she never forgets the nice little things nor is she ever too busy to show her appreciation to other people for what they do for her.

Just a short while ago when I was in Kansas City with my mother who was very ill at the time, Jean did so many things that showed her thoughtfulness. Mr. Bello decided to visit me and the moment Jean knew of his intentions, she made all the arrangements for his reservations and transportation, even to having his berth made up with his head toward the rear of the train, European fashion.

On several occasions I have heard people discuss Jean in my presence without, of course, knowing that I was her mother; and those people have apparently gathered the idea from her screen rôles, that Jean is bold. That is very far from the truth; in fact, she has an inferiority complex. Whenever Jean meets people, she becomes panicky. She goes through the ordeal with grace, but on many occasions I have found that she was so

nervous that her hands were dripping with perspiration.

● ONCE A GIRL asked me if Jean was overbearing with her servants. Not one bit! Each has his or her work to do and if something additional must be done, Jean asks them politely and almost apologetically to do it. The result is that they adore her and try to think of ways and means of pleasing her. If one of them is ill, Jean is deeply concerned and sends her own doctor to them. Whenever a picture of hers is being previewed, she obtains tickets for them all and gives them the evening off.

I suppose many of the young girls who read this article will want to know about Jean's wardrobe. Jean has no particular interest in clothes, except that she be well groomed and dainty. I am sure she has fewer clothes than most girls her age. She wears dark colors, largely blue and black, for street, and white for evening. Her dresses are always the simplest in line that she can buy; and once she finds a frock which she really likes, and that is very seldom, she wears it with different accessories until I wonder it doesn't fall off her in ribbons.

She has only one extravagance—pajamas. She has a dozen or more of them in various colors and materials. That sounds like a great many pajamas but if you knew what a battle it is to get her out of them and into a dress and how seldom I succeed, you would think she probably needed more.

● HER LINGERIE is not made of satin nor silks, as one might suppose. I believe, I have said before, that Jean is fastidious. She has everything that she possibly can in white. Her room, her hangers, her drawers with the little white sachet powders, her shoe-trees, and all the other little things that a girl likes to have in her room.

But to get back to her lingerie, Jean prefers fine white linen, which are very plainly tailored, and I might add that she doesn't care for lace, particularly on her underthings and nighties.

She is very neat about her room and particularly about her wardrobe drawers. Her hand bags are all wrapped in tissue paper before she puts them away. Her gloves are never worn but once without being cleaned. As they come back from the cleaners they are tied in pairs with tiny white ribbon and filed neatly in their particular drawer. Her handkerchiefs and stockings are treated the same way.

When a girl reaches stardom in pictures, it is almost a necessity to have a personal maid. Jean has one, Blanche. However, Jean can and does do many things herself. If she comes out of the pool and her hair is damp, which it always is, it couldn't help but be if you should ever see her swim. I might add, Jean taught herself to swim. She doesn't wait for Blanche to fix it, but does it herself. She always has waved the top of her own hair, and now she rolls the ends up on her fingers and secures it with pins. When she dresses to go out, many times she forgets to tell Blanche. However, I know because she keeps running in and out of my room like a little girl dressing for her first party, and saying, "Do I look all right, Mommie?" And perhaps you have already guessed the answer. She always does look all right, because, after all, though she may be a screen personality to you, she is just a daughter to me.

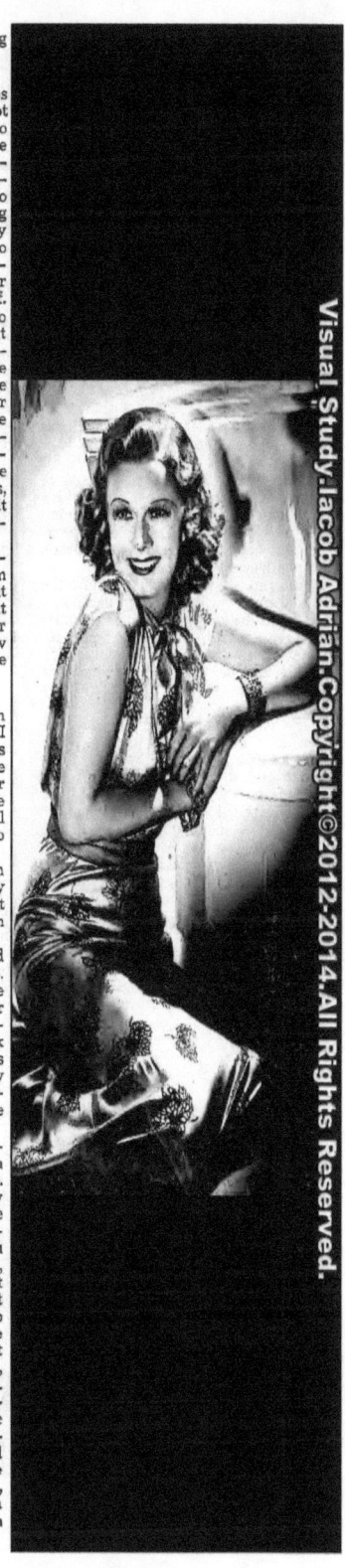

DANGEROUS GAMBLE

thing I realized was that while mother had always been my best friend, and like another girl to me, I had always been the daughter—always running to her for comfort and reassurance, and advice and guidance, like any daughter. Yet on the other hand, I had been making my way professionally in the world for a number of years, standing on my own two feet, fighting my way, on my own, at the studio. Why wasn't I like that at home? Was it because I had grown up so fast on one side of me, that the other side had lagged behind? Then, all in a flash, I knew that I wanted to develop self-sufficiency in my personal life, as well as in my professional one.

● "It's FUNNY . . ." Jean grinned to herself, a nice honest grin. "It's funny, how once you make up your mind to a thing, you must find some expression for the new thought, 'right away, in some way—no matter how. I wanted to show myself that I could handle the reins of my own life, and my own house —so I had the kitchen repainted! Mother had been running everything so perfectly, that the kitchen was the only thing I could discover that needed improvement!" Jean laughed aloud merrily now.

"The next thing I did was to take over the job of planning menus, while mother was away. Little by little, I began to feel that my house was really part of my responsibility, and I liked it. I decided if I liked that responsibility, I might like another. So, later in the fall, after mother had returned, I startled her one day by announcing that now I was the man of the family, and as man of the family, I'd look after the finances, the household budget, and my own expenditures. And what's more, right then and there, I put myself on an allowance.

"Was mother upset? You mean, because I was intruding in what she might have considered her territory? Oh, no,

not a bit of it—and you don't know my mother or you wouldn't have asked that question. I'm really sorry you don't, too, because you'd love her. She was delighted! Oh, I know a lot of mothers consciously, or unconsciously, try to keep their sons and daughters from growing up and becoming self-sufficient, but that's not my mother at all. She has really always looked forward to the day when we'd become two women friends together, not just 'mother and baby.' And I know that day has come. Now she leans on me just as often as I used to lean on her, and when a problem arises we discuss it sensibly and sanely and analytically, and I have the happy feeling that I can be of almost as much help to her, as she is to me."

I interrupted for a moment. "Tell me, Jean—with this growing-up process, have you developed any new ambitions in life?" And it was then that Jean said the truest, most thought-provoking thing I have ever heard a star say:

"Oh, no," she answered quickly. "I have fewer ambitions than I ever had. And I'm happier with the few." Then she leaned forward and explained earnestly. "You see, as a very young girl—like most young girls, I suppose—I wanted and wished for so much, and dreamed of so many triumphs for myself, and dreamed of myself traveling to so many far places, in the far distant future, that I was missing a lot of the simple everyday happiness right here.

● "I'VE DISCOVERED THAT too many ambitions breed discontent. Besides, chasing a *lot* of rainbows scatters your energies, so that you never even capture one. It's difficult to explain, but I guess now I've sort of 'settled down.' I know now that the one thing I want to do is to have better rôles on the screen, and to do better by them, and to live my personal life calmly and maturely. I'm not going to 'flirt' with ideas any

more. If I have what I think is a good one, I'm going to carry it through.

"It was that way about my hair. For a long time I've wanted to change the color of my hair. But when I mentioned it at the studio, I was persuaded against it. My platinum hair had helped make me famous, they said. Better leave well enough alone. But then came my 'turning point'—that day when mother left and I faced myself alone. And as I knew I was putting my youthful gay platinum blonde personality behind me, so I [Continued on page 70]

Your command post-card dictates the contents of our magazine! Write now, naming your favorite

The Command Story

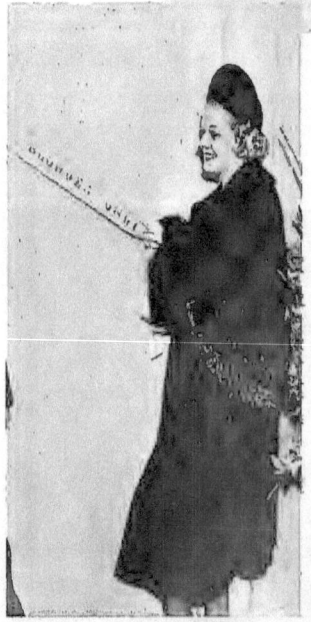

The platinum is gone, but Jean Harlow still rates as a blonde! Max Factor called on her to dedicate the new blonde room of his palatial Hollywood shop right after Jean darkened her hair. It was a gala night

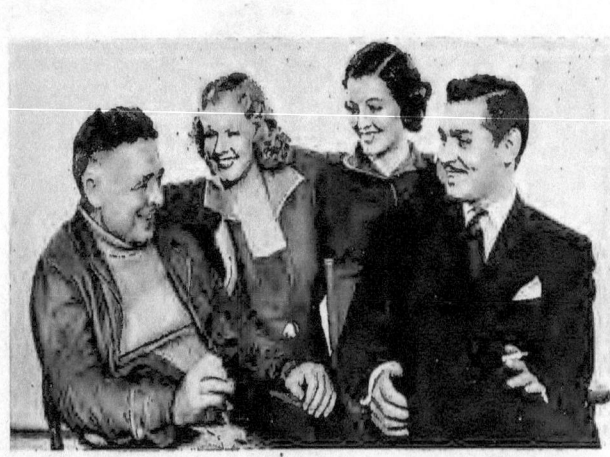

Here's Jean Harlow with her new brownette-style hair, as she appears in *Wife vs Secretary*. Director Clarence Brown, Jean, Myrna Loy, Clark Gable seem happy!

Jean Harlow's Dangerous Gamble

wanted to symbolize it by changing the shade of my hair—and become just a 'normal' blonde. The studio still fought me on it, but I fought back, and I won out. I think the fans will like it. I hope so," she added thoughtfully.

"And I began fighting, too, for a different kind of rôle. For different kind of clothes to wear in pictures. For different, more sedate publicity. I begged and begged for a part in which I wouldn't have to speak bad English, and slink up to 'my man.' And at last I have it! In *Wife Versus Secretary*, the picture I'm doing now with Myrna Loy and Clark Gable, I play the part of an efficient secretary, whose work comes before everything else, and I don't have even one love scene with Clark Gable, and I wear mostly tailored suits and plain little dresses, and I wear only one evening dress in the entire picture!" Jean's enthusiasm was so real, and so triumphant, that I easily understood why she won the battle about her hair, and this new part, even against the studio. Her new determination is the kind of determination that must win out!

● EVEN WHERE ROMANCE is concerned. For a long time, as you know, Jean and Bill Powell have been in love. They drifted along, gayly, happily, finding perfect companionship, each in the other. Everyone thought it would lead to marriage. So, perhaps, did Jean and Bill. Until along came the time when Jean found herself facing facts squarely—(and that means, maturing)! Until along came the day when Jean decided to slough off a few of the ambitions and distant desires which were diverting her thoughts and her 'drive'—and narrow down to one or two instead. And most important, was the necessity of rebuilding her career along new lines. It wasn't a necessity where her fans or her box office was concerned. But where the new Jean herself was concerned, it was vital. Tackling a new career and a marriage at the same time, she wisely concluded would be difficult, if not impossible. Career won out. And so now, while Jean and Bill still hold each other in high regard, while they still see each other in the same old gay, glorious way, the marriage angle seems to be out.

● BUT EVEN THEN, "dates" occupy only a small part of her time these days—and even less of her mind. There's the new kind of reading for example. Jean has always read a lot, but she admits that while she used to read for entertainment, and to "kill time," she now reads with an entirely different attitude to learn and study and be well-informed. "A year ago," she said, "I wouldn't have thought of re-reading a book, because I used to read only for the story. But now I find it interesting to read and re-read, trying to analyze an author's style, and I always find something in a second reading that I missed in the first."

I guessed that this new interest in reading also had something to do with Jean's writing, and when I asked her, she said, "Yes, I've taken my book, *Today Is Tonight*, off the shelf again, and

I'm rewriting parts of it, and doing a lot of editing. The truth of the matter is that I've never even submitted it to a publisher, because up until now, I've been afraid to. I had no confidence in it. But when I get through working this time, I will! Because I feel so much more steady and calm in my own mind, that I'm sure my book will reflect it. More than anything, I guess, I've developed *perspective*. I can stand off and look at things as they are, not as they seem to be.

"I can even do that with myself these days. One of the things I discovered needed correcting in me was my frankness. Frankness is something that I never purposely developed. It's always been part of me—something I couldn't help. I never weighed one answer against another—but always, answered as I felt, even when I was talking to an interviewer. Well, I still believe that honesty is the best policy—but I've learned that sometimes my frankness has been misinterpreted as boldness, and so now I've learned to curb it a bit, and to speak with more deliberation."

● ANOTHER CHANGE that has come over Jean is one that she didn't tell me about, but one that others have mentioned. And that is the change in her attitude of generosity. Jean has always been the kind of girl who would give you the shirt off her back—and usually did, figuratively, if not literally. If you were a friend of Jean's, or even just an acquaintance, and happened to admire a pair of hose she was wearing, Jean would probably say, "I just bought several dozen of these . . . come up to the house and I'll give you a dozen."

Well, Jean is still generous, even more so, but she is directing her generosity in different directions. She suddenly realized that all her giving was usually to satisfy a whim—hers, or another person's—and that she wasn't always giving where giving would do the most good. A dozen pair of hose, or an evening dress, or a bracelet, after all, were luxury gifts. Now Jean tries to give only to the needy, and to give them the things that will make their lives more comfortable, and their tummies fuller.

The interesting thing is that all these changes have become reflected in Jean's face. Her face is softer, prettier, happier than I have ever seen it. Jean's eyes have always looked everyone straight in the eyes—but now they seem to be even more calm and steady than ever. Her smile is still quick to flash, but it has a warm quality it never had before. So is her body more beautiful and more poised than ever. And her hair—

But I almost forgot! One of the things that Jean has demanded as a part of her change in publicity is that it be straight to the point—minus frills and furbelows and a lot of palaver about "the sun streaming through the window, turning the bright glint of her hair to silver flame."

"It's because I don't want people to think of how I look anymore," she said with spirit. "There's been too much of that. They looked at me as I was on the screen, all gleaming satin, and brass and brazen, and so thought I was like that in person. Well, I'm not. So if you think I've said anything that's interesting, or helpful, or important, write it down—but forget about the descriptive adjectives."

So, I guess . . . I'll just let it go at that!

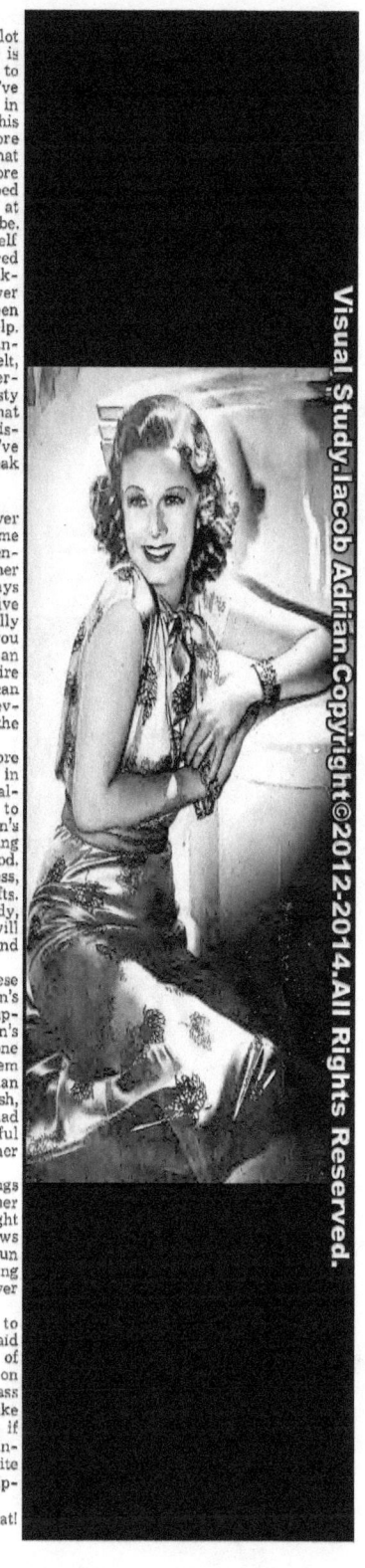

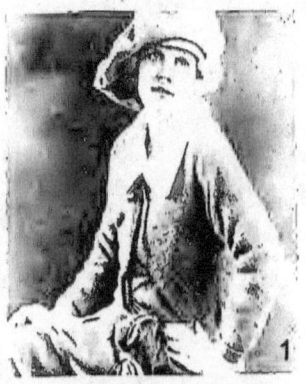

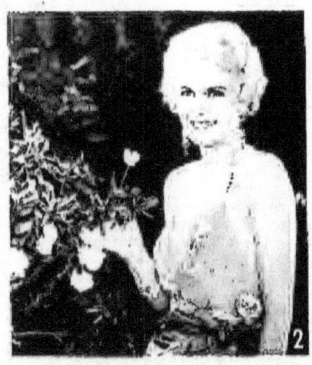

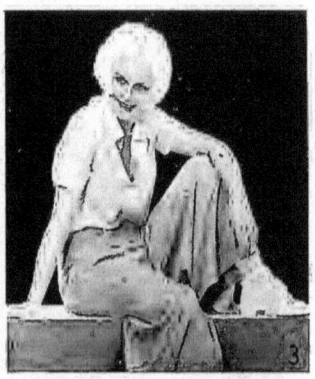

Jean Carpenter, they called her in Kansas City. The Glamour wasn't very impressive

Jean Harlow, Hollywood's latest Cinderella. That's how they billed her for *Hell's Angels*

1931 . . . Jean looked like this as Fox prepared to offer the production, *Goldie*

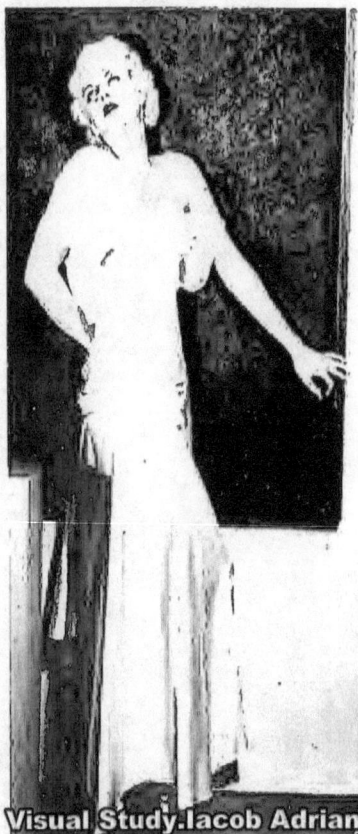

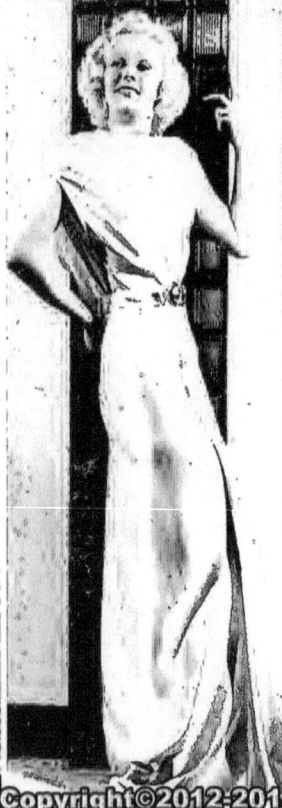

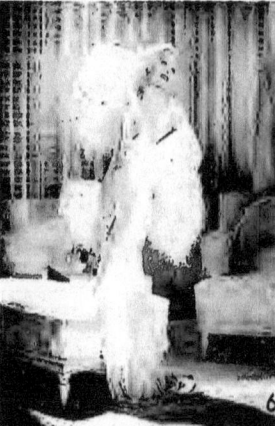

Dinner at Eight, Girl from Missouri, Reckless, China Seas—hit after hit

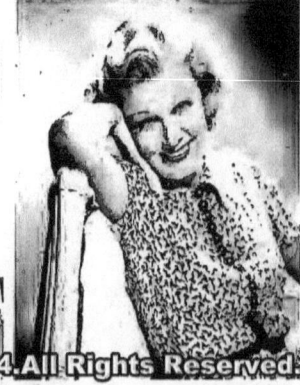

Ah, this is beginning to look familiar! Jean acquired her first glamour with Caddo company

Sophistication—M·G·M's gift to Jean Harlow. Her glamour took on new depth, the toast of the fans

1936 . . . and a Harlow revolution! Gone the platinum blonde of old. High voltage eyes replace low cut gowns and the fans still cheer

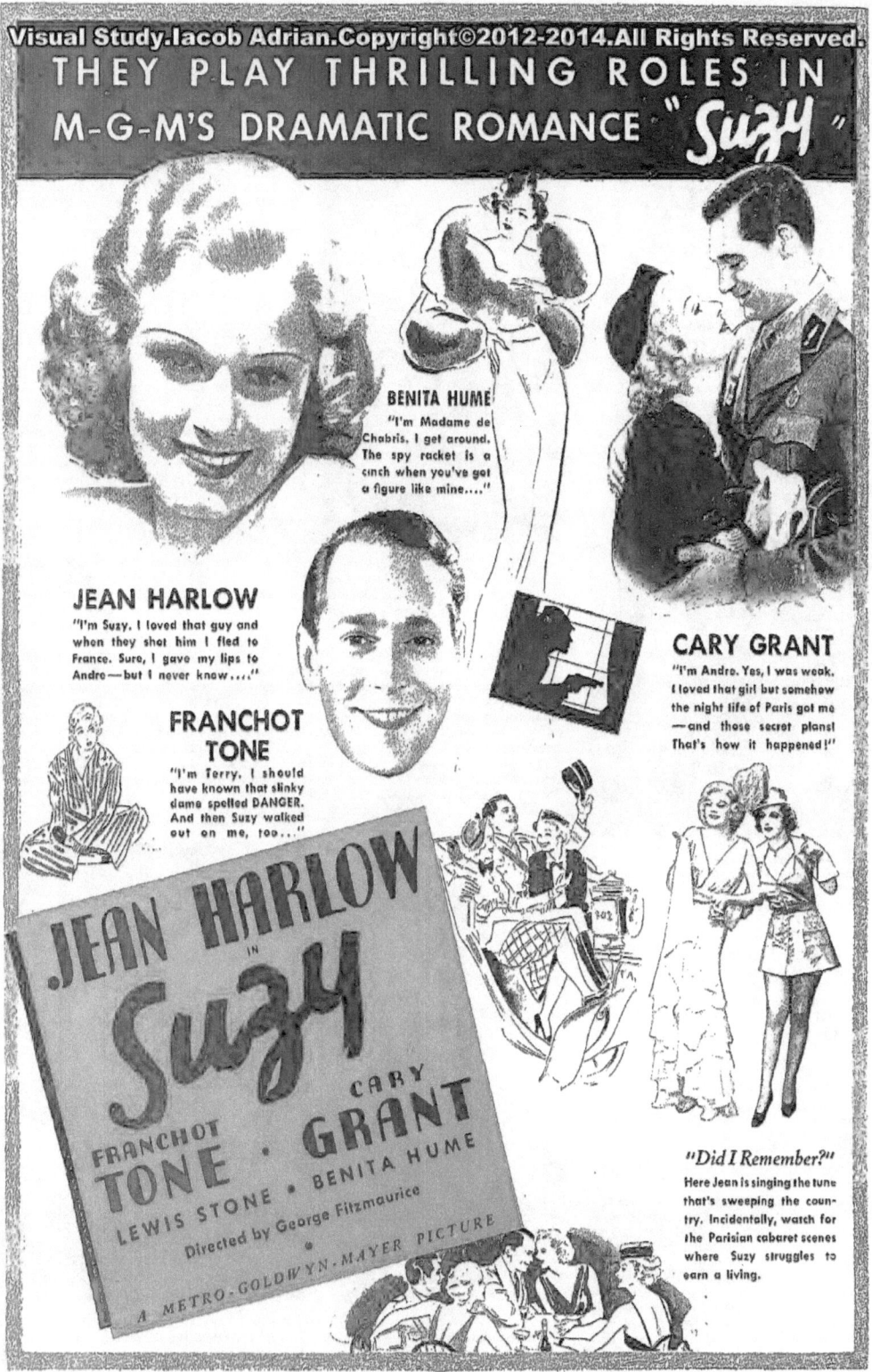

THEY PLAY THRILLING ROLES IN
M-G-M'S DRAMATIC ROMANCE "Suzy"

BENITA HUME
"I'm Madame de Chabris, I get around. The spy racket is a cinch when you've got a figure like mine...."

JEAN HARLOW
"I'm Suzy, I loved that guy and when they shot him I fled to France. Sure, I gave my lips to Andre—but I never knew...."

CARY GRANT
"I'm Andre. Yes, I was weak, I loved that girl but somehow the night life of Paris got me —and those secret plans! That's how it happened!"

FRANCHOT TONE
"I'm Terry, I should have known that slinky dame spelled DANGER. And then Suzy walked out on me, too..."

JEAN HARLOW
IN
Suzy
FRANCHOT TONE · CARY GRANT
LEWIS STONE · BENITA HUME
Directed by George Fitzmaurice
A METRO-GOLDWYN-MAYER PICTURE

"Did I Remember?"
Here Jean is singing the tune that's sweeping the country. Incidentally, watch for the Parisian cabaret scenes where Suzy struggles to earn a living.

If You Knew Suzy, Like I Know Suzy

"IF YOU KNEW Suzy, like I know Suzy . . ."

Who is Suzy? Suzy is Jean Harlow. At least, the Jean Harlow on the screen. In her new M-G-M picture, *Suzy*, you will see Jean a little as you knew her in *Hell's Angels*—a little like the *Red Dust* Jean, but that isn't the point. I want you to know Jean, as I know Jean.

I have known her a long time. As an actress, and as a friend.

They call her "Baby." She is a baby because she likes to sleep 14 hours a day; likes fuzzy kittens, picnics, orchids, licking the frosting dish, reading the funnies, seeing Mickey Mouse.

She is NOT a baby, because—she has a good sound philosophy of life and living. No one puts a thing over on her. She is a good friend, and a dependable one. She will never let you down. She has a marvelous sense of humor—even when the joke is on her. Jean believes that you have to work for what you get out of life —but that there is no use making a complex struggle out of it.

She is a walking contradiction. Jean

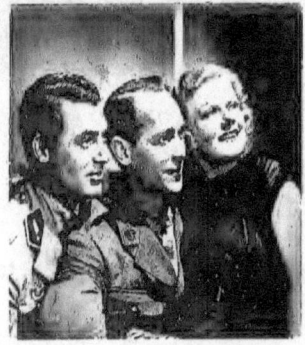

An unusual photo study of three unusual head-liners, all of whom contribute to the success of the film, Suzy, Cary Grant, Franchot Tone and Jean Harlow

has moods. Sometimes she believes them, sometimes she wants you to believe them. She is a girl who takes a sincere joy in the problems of her friends. She falls in and out of headlines, unwittingly, yet is a too-sympathetic little girl.

She Loves to Sleep

● PEOPLE DON'T LIKE To believe the best about Jean, and she knows it. They are continually saying "now tell us what she is *really* like."

But if you knew Jean, like I know Jean, these are some of the things that you would know.

She often falls to sleep—not because she is bored, but because she may be tired— and loves to sleep. A perfect date to her is packing a huge picnic hamper (the old-fashioned kind) and going away into the hills or near the ocean. Night clubs are fun to Jean once in a while, but not often. She loves to go fishing. Often she will charter a boat, pile a few of her real friends on it, and go off for the day. She baits her own hooks, and doesn't wrinkle

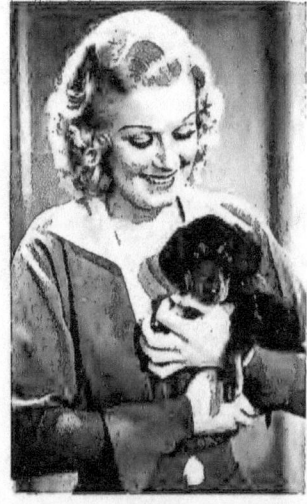

Meet Adolph-the-Flying-Dutchman! He is one of Jean Harlow's many pets. Read about her assortment of dogs and cats in this revealing story of the star of M-G-M's film, Suzy

up her nose and look dainty about it.

Jean has two huge Persian cats. She adores them. They are very aristocratic cats, and often ignore their mistress because they are in a mood. When they want to be praised they catch a mouse, march up to Jean's bedroom with it.

The cats have no names. They look so much alike that Jean can't tell them apart. There is no use naming them. They have breakfast with Jean every morning.

Jean always puts them out at night; that is her last job of the day. One time they had a hole cagily torn in a corner of the screen, and came in as fast as she put them out. She was putting out cats for some time, before she discovered their game. When they know it is time to go out, they hide, and it is her job to find them. Since they are as much alike as Ike and Mike, she sometimes wonders if she is not repeating.

Jean hates to be alone. People need not be around her to talk—just to be there. She is never idle. When she rides to and from the studio, or wherever she is going, she usually reads. She reads constantly. When she is not working and has time, she reads consistently. Good books. When she is working, she sends Blanche, her colored maid, over to the studio library to get a book. Any book. It might be a heavy volume of history or a murder mystery. She wants to read all kinds of books, like she wants to know all kinds of people. She always finishes a book, once she starts it. It is a matter of discipline with her.

And She's Domestic!

● WHEN SHE Is having her hair done at the studio it is usually while she is eating her breakfast, reading, answering the phones and talking about costumes. She has an amazing faculty for doing more than one thing at once.

Jean is domestic. She loves to have complete charge of the house. She is surrounded by a retinue of colored servants who adore her, and are too willing to carry out her every order. When her mother left for a visit to Kansas City, Jean had the kitchen re-painted, she de-mothed the drapes and rugs, had walls cleaned, new tile in the bathroom, and was just too busy!

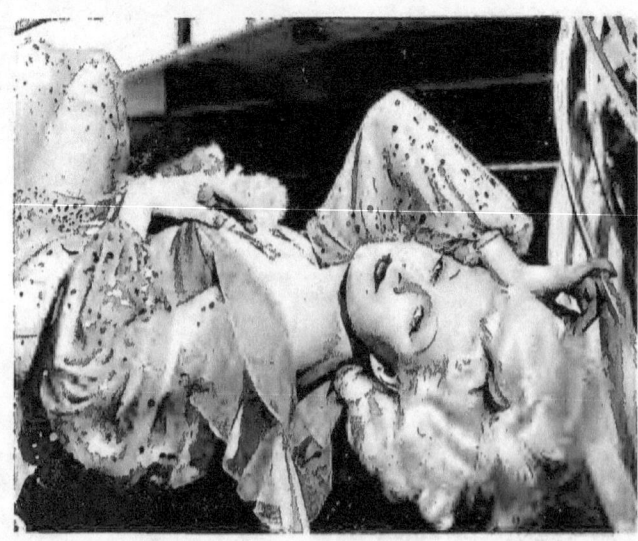

And this is the Jean Harlow you used to know—totally different from the purposeful young lady in the above photos! It was a type of rôle she cordially hated, and condemned as soon as she could make herself heard

If You Knew Suzy, Like I Know Suzy

And she can cook. Everything from pies to a regular meal. We have a mutual friend who has a very modest little house, and a six-year-old son. She likes to visit her, get up and get breakfast, then go into the backyard and play mud pies with the six-year-old. She doesn't mind doing dishes—even remembers to clean the stove!

Jean takes her sports in flings. She will go in for golf in a very serious manner. About the fifth hole, it will be more fun to sit in the shade of a hazard and talk to her partner.

She likes to ride. Takes it up seriously—for a couple of weeks.

Luxury Always Welcome

● ALONG WITH ALL THIS, she loves luxury. She won't create it for herself, but likes it. Lovely flowers, mirrored dressing room, luxurious bedroom, a cabinet of perfumes. But she forgets them as soon as she walks away from them. Her gloves are kept in very neat order, wrapped in tissue paper. Her bureau drawers are perfectly arranged, except for one bottom one where she flings things. That is called her "procrastination drawer."

She has cupboards of neatly arranged shoes. Shoes—size three—for every occasion and costume. She loves shoes. No other article of clothing matters to her. She hates to shop, and is not clothes-conscious. Her mother and close friends have to shop for her.

Jean is fun on a party, though she thinks that she is a perfect flop—and hates them. She is fun because she is interested in other people. She is terrorized at the thought of big gatherings. Gets a terrific inferiority complex. That is the reason that she sometimes has the "hello fellows" attitude, to hide it.

Jean has a way of talking you into things. You will approach her with all sorts of good reasons why she should do a certain thing. It is not until you are a couple of blocks away from her when you realize your point was lost in the shuffle—and you wonder if you were right in the first place.

She starts her morning with a glass of hot water and lemon juice. At first because she thought it was good for her, and now because she likes it.

Draws the Maternal Instinct

● PEOPLE WANT To look after Jean and take care of her. To Blanche, her colored maid who has been with her for six years, Jean is her whole life. Jean never has to ask Blanche to do a thing. Blanche has a silent way of taking care of Jean, seeing that people do not tire her, that she wears the right dress for the occasion, and eats properly. When Jean is tired from a day's work, she will ask Blanche to bring her a bowl of soup. Blanche will say, "Yes, Miss Jean." Then appear again with a tray of good warm vegetables, a lamb chop, and glass of milk. Jean looks at her, sighs, but knows that it will stay there until she eats it. She does, and feels better.

If Jean wants to wear slacks to a studio conference, Blanche is very sorry but they are at the cleaners. All twelve pairs. Jean wears a smart sports outfit. When she gets home from the studio—she can slip into comfortable slacks, laid out on the bed—just arrived from the cleaners.

Jean doesn't mind autograph seekers. She says that she is grateful for their interest.

Jean is a very concrete person. A very loyal person. She keeps a promise, once she makes one. Yet she is a terrific procrastinator. She is careful of the promises she makes.

You can depend upon Jean to keep a secret. She is one girl to whom you can tell anything. She gives good, sound advice, and doesn't forget your problem the next time you see her. It is not a "personality interest" as so many people affect.

At the present time Jean has a two-and-a-half-pound Pomeranian (to take the place of the Great Dane that died), three bunnies, four cats, a Dachshund, and what else I don't know, because I haven't seen her for a week.

Color Scheme is Simple

● HER FAVORITE COLORS (only they aren't colors) are black and white. White men like, and black is always smart. She has a temper—and a good one. It is a justifiable one. Not one that flares up for no reason at all. But when it does—watch out. Never expect to fool her or neglect to fulfill a promise, and think she will forget it—because she won't. She expects the same loyalty that she gives. She doesn't hold a grudge—you just don't exist to her any more.

Jean has few friends. Friendship is sacred to her. She has many acquaintances, but friendship is something that takes time, trouble and thought. She knows people, and does not misplace her friendship. On first meeting, Jean can tell what sort of a person you are. She hates insincerity above everything else.

Jean likes to form her own opinions. If you try to influence her, or talk her into things, you are beaten before you start. So don't try.

Jean is capable. She knows how to sew. She can shampoo and wave her own hair. She can mix up a supper out of nothing and everything—all her own concoctions. She is not spoiled, with all of the attention she has—but loves to spoil other people.

Left Out of a Party

● JEAN LOVES TO SURPRISE people, and play gags. One time when a friend of hers (a very good one) neglected to invite Jean to a dinner party—Jean went anyway. It was a formal party. Jean arrived in slacks, brought her own picnic supper, and sat on the living room floor to eat it, nonchalantly disposing of egg shells over her shoulder, and had a grand time. The party was a success, because of the uninvited guest.

Music—everything from Beethoven to Crosby—according to the mood. She still loves "The Music Goes Round and Round."

Jean always makes an entrance everywhere she goes. I still don't know whether or not she is conscious of it. Whether she is being a movie star or is self-conscious. (I'll tell you when I find out.)

Jean is one of those daughters all mothers dream about. She comes home from a date, wakes her mother up, and tells her things.

She is interested in her fan mail. I'm glad I know Suzy,

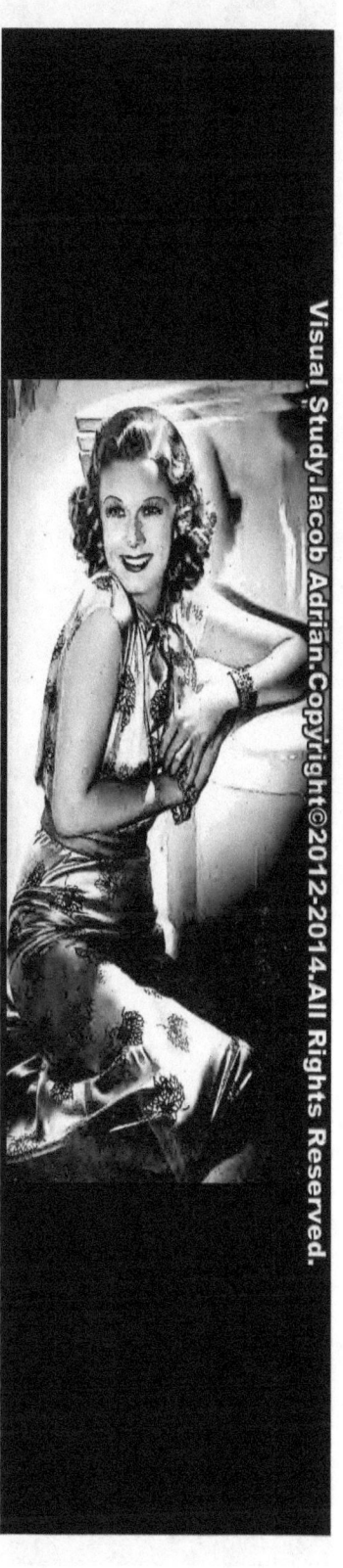

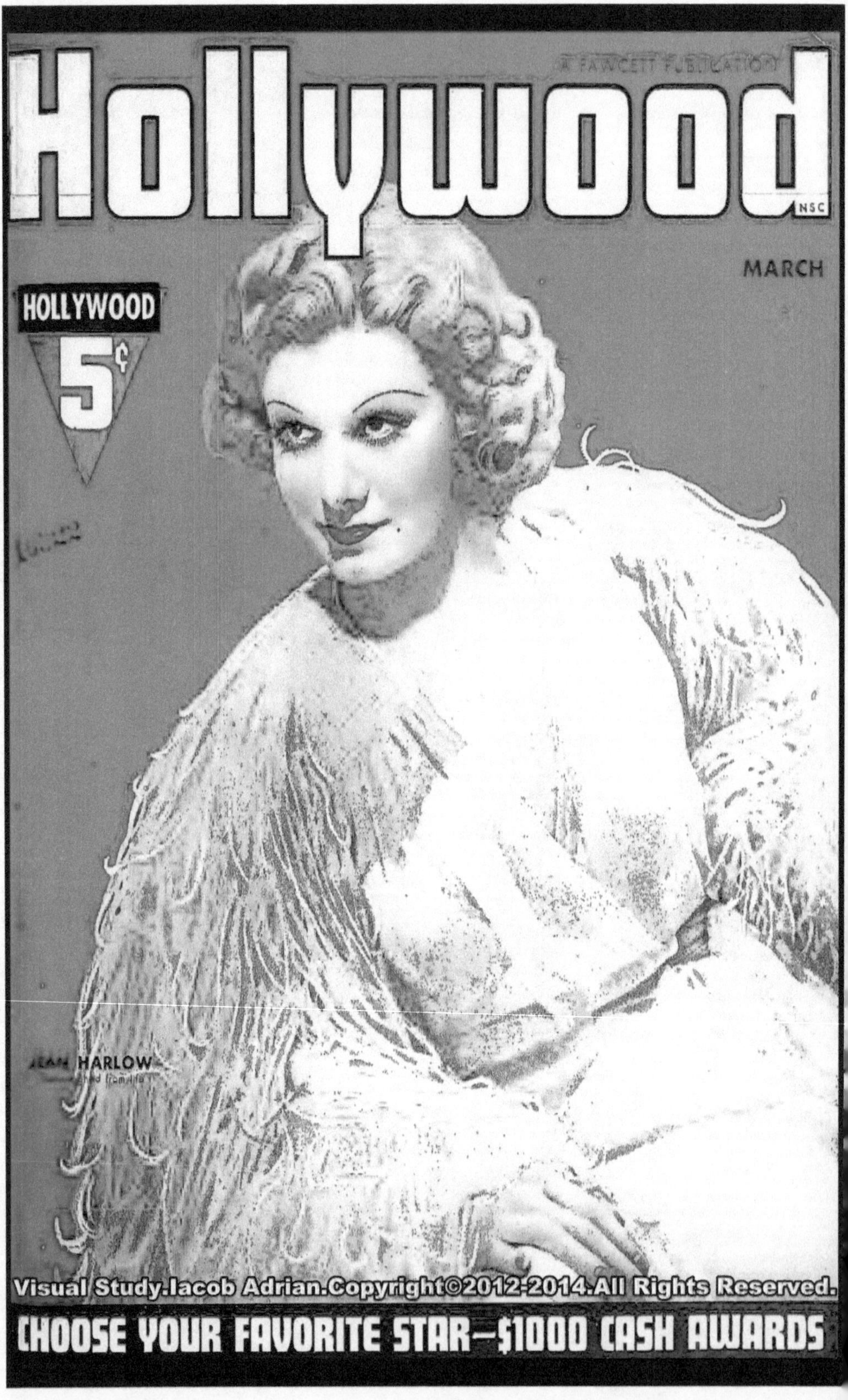
A FAWCETT PUBLICATION
Hollywood
NSC
MARCH
HOLLYWOOD
5¢
JEAN HARLOW
Visual Study.Iacob Adrian.Copyright©2012-2014.All Rights Reserved.
CHOOSE YOUR FAVORITE STAR—$1000 CASH AWARDS

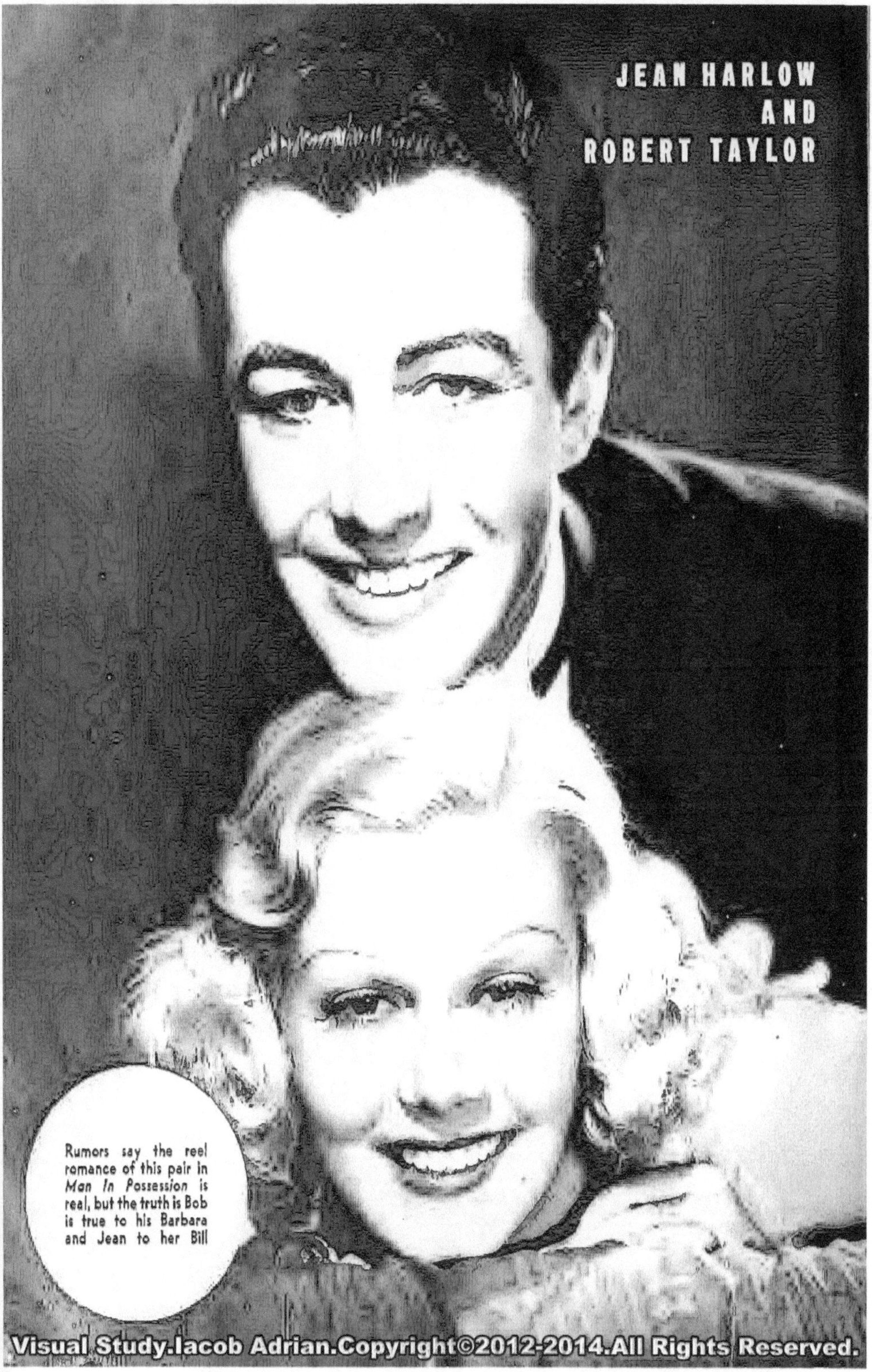

JEAN HARLOW
AND
ROBERT TAYLOR

Rumors say the reel
romance of this pair in
Man In Possession is
real, but the truth is Bob
is true to his Barbara
and Jean to her Bill

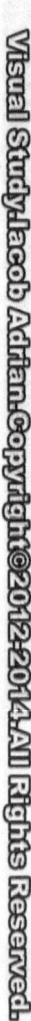

Preview of their first picture together!

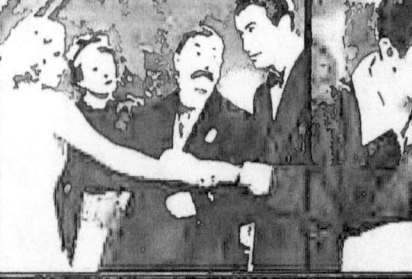
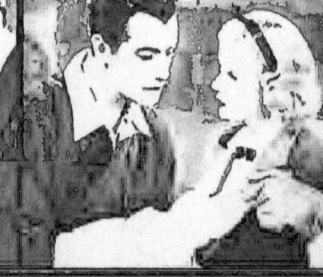

How Bob loves — and how Jean loves it!...It's a merry mad farce in the M·G·M "Libeled Lady" manner — which means high-powered romance mixed in with the laughs!...Here's the merriest of Springtime pictures!

Bob is assigned by the sheriff to guard Jean's personal property...that's when the fun begins!

He masquerades as her butler, so her high-toned society friends won't suspect she's flat broke...

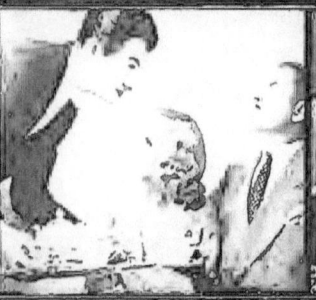
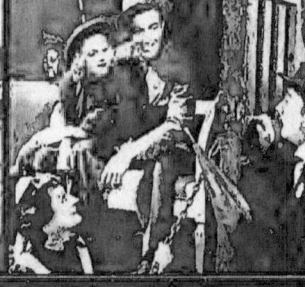

Who should Jean's honor-guest be but Bob's fortune-hunting brother, who thinks Jean is an heiress!

Bob's the boy to clear up complications — so he becomes Jean's personal property, Item No. 1

JEAN   ROBERT

HARLOW · TAYLOR

in

"Personal Property"

with **Reginald Owen**

A Metro-Goldwyn-Mayer Picture · Produced by John W. Considine, Jr.

Directed by **W. S. VAN DYKE**

The Hit-Director of "After the Thin Man" "San Francisco" and others

How Jean Is Breaking

By Mark Dowling

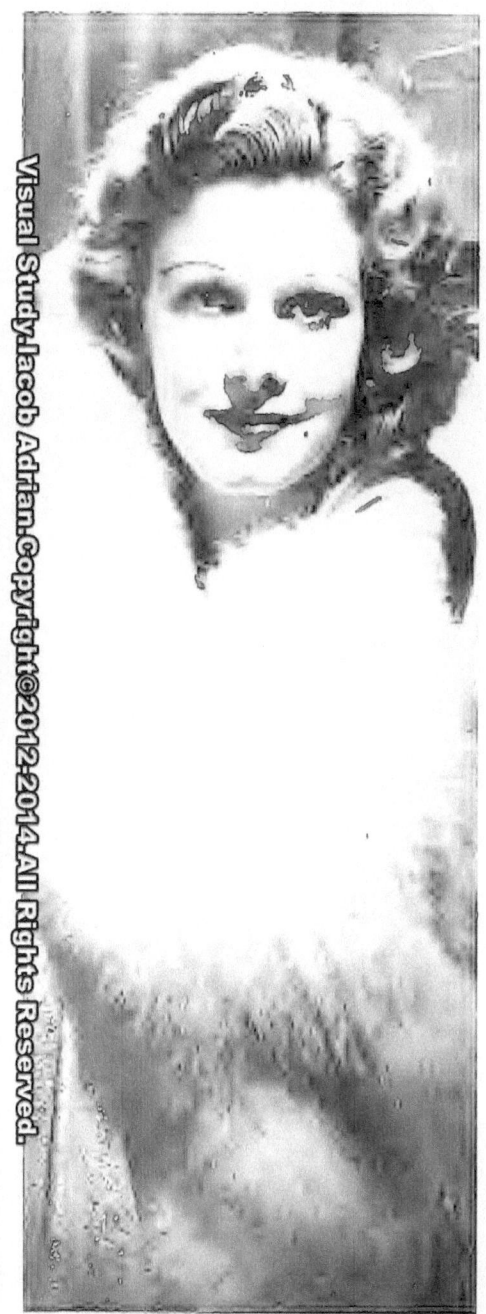

Today the lovely Jean is making a new bid for fame in which histrionic ability takes precedence over the hydra-headed sex elements that once were her chief stocks in trade. Gone is the platinum tresses, carefully concealed are the svelte curves, but her charms still sing

O NE YEAR AGO Jean Harlow made me a promise.

"There'll be no more bombshells for me—if I can possibly prevent them."

She added softly, "Once and for all, I'm going to smash the Harlow jinx."

Then Jean explained how she has kept that promise, avoiding headlines and sensational events for one year. She also explained what she meant by the Harlow jinx—a sort of destiny for attracting trouble.

"As a little girl, playing with my friends on a rainy day, I was always the one who fell in the mud puddle. And the first time a boy ever tried to kiss me—I was seven, I think, or maybe six—I reached back one arm and socked him. Socked so hard," she grinned ruefully, "that when he ducked, I gave *myself* a bloody nose.

"At boarding school," she added, "I remember being singled out for questioning whenever some minor prank was committed, though as a matter of fact I was pretty darned serious about my studies and general conduct."

As she grew to womanhood, an amazing destiny of adventure and misfortune followed Jean, with an avalanche of headlines and notoriety at every climax of her tempestuous life.

"I used to be sorry," she told me. "I used to be afraid. I wondered *why* things always happened to me.

"Then suddenly I realized that being sorry is dodging life, not living it. It's when you say, instead, 'I'm going to think this through, and get to the bottom of it!' that your problems begin to solve themselves.

"That's the slogan I adopted when I made the promise," Jean explained. "It works! I hate to think of the headlines that might have smeared my name all over the papers if I hadn't stopped to think things out—and made myself, really, the master instead of the tool of my own destiny!"

Right now, Jean told us, reporters are telephoning her intimate friends both day and night, hounding them with questions regarding Jean's rumored romance with Bob Taylor.

Members of the cast of *Personal Property* have been forced to disconnect their phones to avoid the hammering questions of Hollywood's three-hundred-odd reporters, syndicate writers, columnists and radio chatterers.

"Is it true that Bob Taylor has lunch every day in Harlow's dressing room?"

"Did Bill Powell visit the *Personal Property* set yesterday and stage a fist fight with Bob Taylor over Jean?"

"Are Harlow and Taylor really planning to elope to Washington together?"

Once all this might have upset Jean to the point of uttering frantic and useless denials. Now she thinks things through—and says nothing.

She told me, sitting before the mirror in her miniature portable dressing room, "I've learned, you see, that it isn't enough just to be right in your own mind. You have to plan so that other people know you're right, too. So now I avoid even the slightest chance of arousing gossip.

"The studio had planned to send Bob and me to Washington to the Inaugural Ball. It had been arranged for us to go on the same train, with a party of other players and press representatives. Harmless enough, wasn't it? But I asked them to change the schedule and let me go by a later train to dodge even the merest possibility of reading about 'a new romance for Harlow.'"

Such caution and forethought may seem exaggerated, but it's just a single instance of the way Jean has learned to handle situations that might have been dynamite.

As for Bill Powell's feelings, he made the perfect answer to a well-known correspondent who had written that he sent a daily box of gardenias to Jean on the set—to keep her from forgetting him despite the presence of the handsome Bob.

While we were chatting, a box of gardenias *did* arrive for Jean—the first Bill had sent her during the production. The card read, wittily, "*Just living up to my press notices . . .*"

Jean's mother told me: "Jean has only gone out in the evening three times in the last nine months. As soon as a production is over, she goes out of town. Not to flashy places like Palm Springs or Santa Barbara, but to some fairly quiet place like Arrowhead where she can really rest, ride, read or hike. She hasn't been to Santa Anita once this season—and she only went twice last year. She sold the big house and has moved into a smaller and less pretentious one. She never goes to parties. She really lives such a prosaic life for a girl of her age that I often urge her to

The Harlow Jinx . . . .

go out and have fun. The answer is always the same, 'Then, if there's any trouble, it'll be laid at my door.' . . . *And perhaps she's right.*"

So if you've pictured Hollywood's most romantic couple, Bill Powell and Jean Harlow, dashing to night clubs, throwing huge parties, or visiting the newest bars, you're wrong—you and a couple of hundred columnists!

They may still print stories about Jean and Bill dancing at the Troc until the early hours and they may even tell you the details of Jean's evening gown—but the way Jean and Bill really spend an evening together is much more amusing and unexpected.

"Sometimes," Jean told me, "after we've both worked late, we'll have dinner in my dressing room on trays. Barbara Brown, my friend and stand-in, joins us. My colored maid serves. I won't have any make-up on and I'll be munching away at the vegetables and other healthy things I try to eat during pictures.

"Every now and then, I'll mutter something pretty glum about my work—a bit of business I'm having difficulty with. Bill gives a grunt of sympathy. He won't be spruced up, either, and the debonair Mr. Powell you know on the screen will have vanished completely.

"After dinner, he may mutter, 'G'night,' and leave without another word. I understand perfectly—friendship and companionship is sometimes great enough to rise above petty gallantries and politeness."

Jean laughed at the unromantic picture she had drawn. Then she added seriously, "Honestly, I love the quiet and comfort I've enjoyed recently. Through *planning* it that way. I've had so much of the other, that there's a thrill in the very uneventfulness of my recent life. It's given me time to catch my breath—to catch up with myself.

"Before, things happened so fast that I hadn't time to evaluate or to plan. All I could do was to pull myself together and gasp, 'Here I am—what do we do next?'"

[Continued on page 65]

Jean blossomed forth ever more alluring as she pursued her screen climb for Metro-Goldwyn-Mayer. No opportunity was overlooked to accentuate sex as personified by the No. 1 platinum blonde. The stigma became a jinx that followed her during her early career

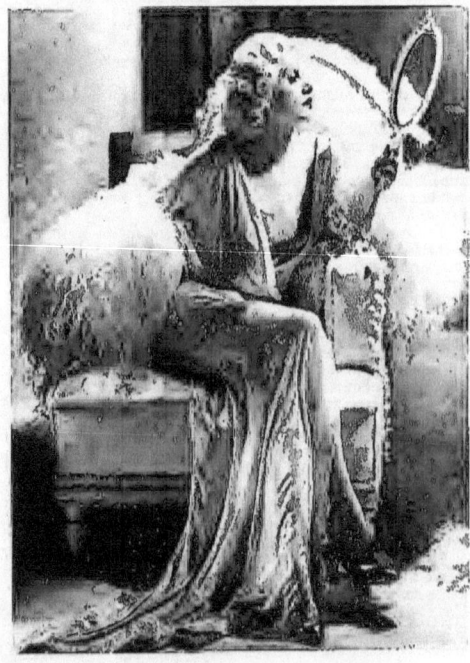

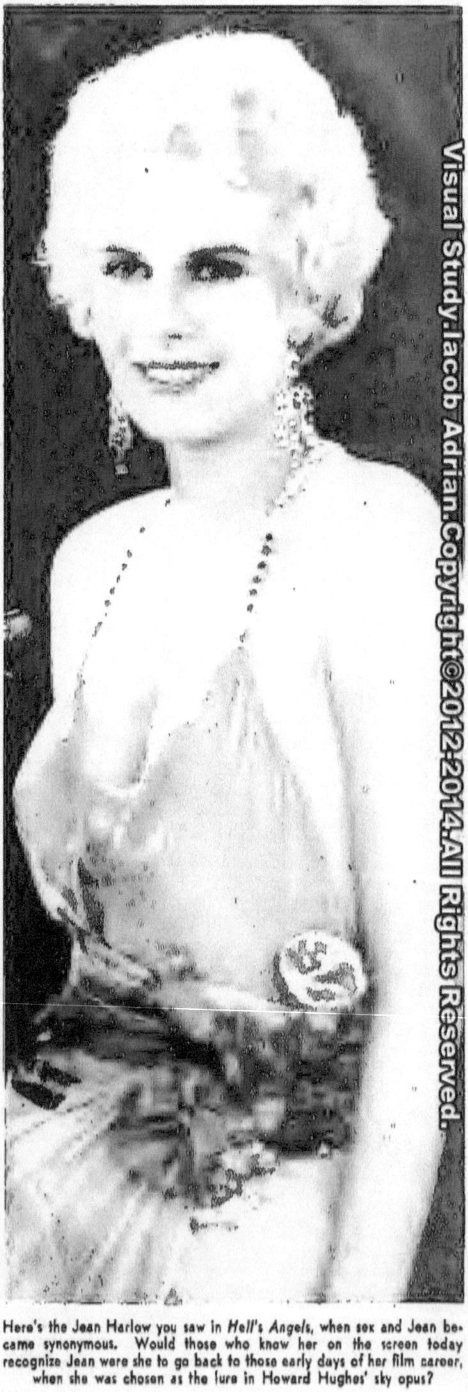

Here's the Jean Harlow you saw in *Hell's Angels*, when sex and Jean became synonymous. Would those who know her on the screen today recognize Jean were she to go back to those early days of her film career, when she was chosen as the lure in Howard Hughes' sky opus?

How Jean is Breaking The Jinx

She added, "Going slower has been good for me as a person—and invaluable to me as an actress. I believe, sincerely, that my work has improved. If you live artificially, your characterizations will be unreal. A famous director once said, 'You're only as good as your last picture in Hollywood!'

"As to the future—I won't attempt to make plans. Nothing I've ever planned in my whole life has worked out, with regard to people, or a pattern of life. I've been planning to go to New York every two months for a year, and I'm still in Hollywood.

"It's the things in the back of my mind, the big things, that are beginning to come true for me. Consciously and subconsciously I've worked to better myself in my profession. They tell me at the studio that it's beginning to show."

In *Libeled Lady* critics singled out Jean's performance for special mention in a cast that included such rivals for attention as Spencer Tracy, Myrna Loy, and Ol' Massa Powell himself!

According to studio reports, *Personal Property*, opposite Bob Taylor, offers Jean the best chance of her career.

"I feel the future is a good deal like walking from one room to another," she told me. "We see the same windows, the same walls, maybe even the same type of furnishing. It's the way we react to things that makes a progression."

There is more than one word of wisdom in what the beautiful and talented Jean says. Progression is the way one re-acts to things—not only external but internal things. That Jean has taken this attitude speaks well for what the future has in store for her. And it can safely be said that her new re-actions explain why, right now, she has conquered, successfully and forever, the "Harlow jinx."

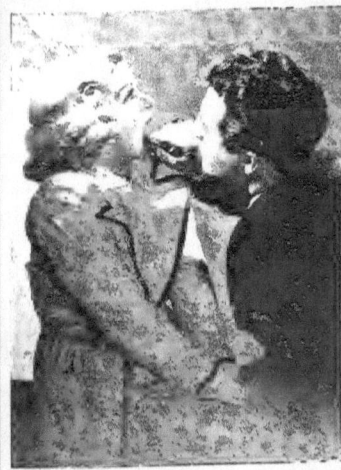

You may wonder as did the editor just what it is that is holding the attention of Robert Taylor. It might be a tooth and it might be a tonsil but with Jean before one, who cares? They co-starred in *Personal Property*

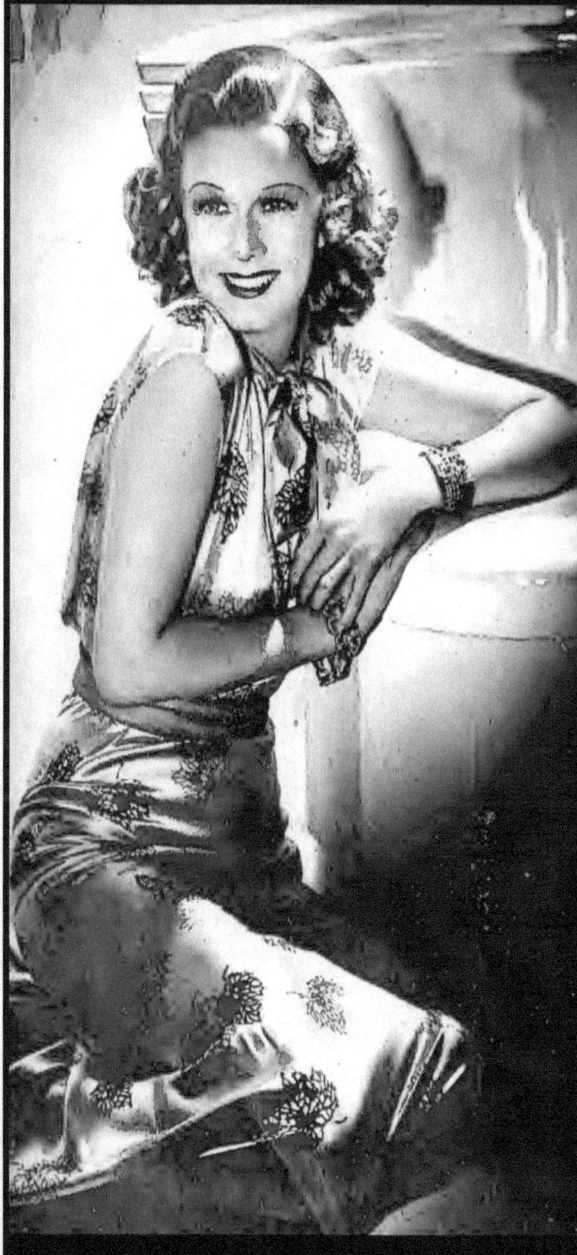

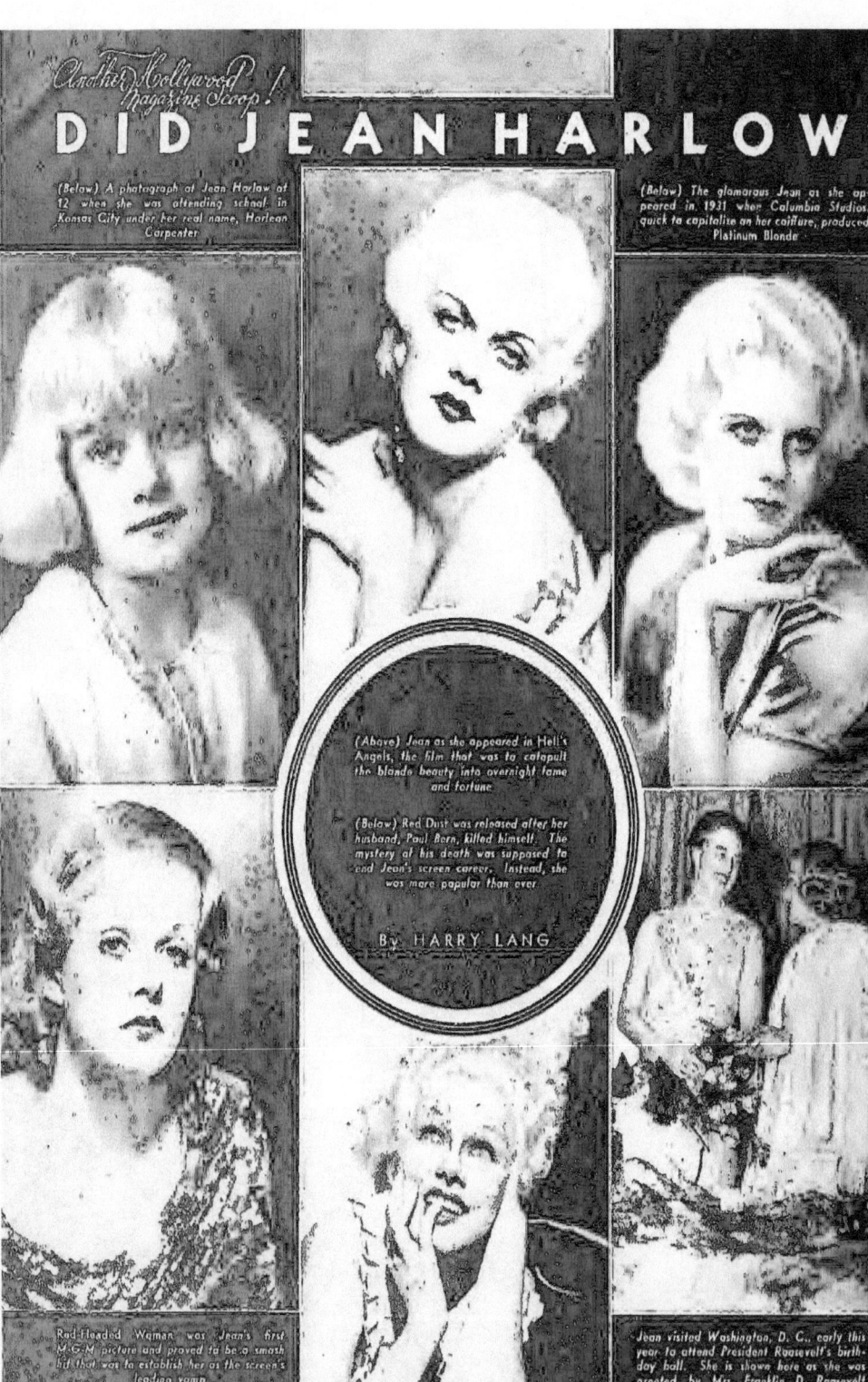

DID JEAN HARLOW

(Below) A photograph of Jean Harlow at 12 when she was attending school in Kansas City under her real name, Harlean Carpenter

(Below) The glamorous Jean as she appeared in 1931 when Columbia Studios, quick to capitalize on her coiffure, produced Platinum Blonde

(Above) Jean as she appeared in Hell's Angels, the film that was to catapult the blonde beauty into overnight fame and fortune

(Below) Red Dust was released after her husband, Paul Bern, killed himself. The mystery of his death was supposed to end Jean's screen career. Instead, she was more popular than ever.

By HARRY LANG

Red-Headed Woman was Jean's first M-G-M picture and proved to be a smash hit that was to establish her as the screen's leading vamp.

Jean visited Washington, D. C., early this year to attend President Roosevelt's birthday ball. She is shown here as she was greeted by Mrs. Franklin D. Roosevelt

HAVE A PREMONITION?

CALL it simply "premonition," if you wish.
Or call it, rather, a brave-hearted resignation to a cruel destiny she somehow, subconsciously perhaps, recognized as inevitable, inescapable—

For Jean Harlow knew, even before that final, fatal illness set upon her, that Death was going to cheat her at last of the final fruition of a happiness she'd sought so vainly throughout her strange young life!

"Child of Sorrow," she'd gone through three disastrous love adventures, in her woman's quest for the man to fill her life. Then, she met Bill Powell—and there flamed at last in her life the love, the comradeship, the fullness of an ideal love. Yet Jean Harlow knew, even as it burst upon her, that that love was doomed!

"With Bill," she told an intimate friend, just a few weeks before her death, "I've found everything I'd never found before. It makes up for all that's happened to me. . . .

"And when it ends—as it probably must, tomorrow, or the tomorrow after that—well, even then I won't feel that life has cheated me—too much."

Amazing prophecy, that. And it's not one of those things that were told *after* her passing. It was told me even before her illness, by the young man to whom Jean confided.

SCION of one of California's richest, oldest families, he is. It was at a mountain week-end house party, on a millionaire's estate, that Jean Harlow talked to him—talked as she rarely talked even to intimates. Somehow, between her and this young man, one of those sudden close friendships "clicked," like that. No love, no romance—just palship. And one day, as they walked ankle deep in pine needles, far from the house party crowd, Jean felt moved to confidences.

She told of her three marriages, and of the sorrow that went with them. She told things that, in fairness to others, cannot ever be repeated, now. But she opened her heart, and told the inside of the story all Hollywood knows—and you know, too. Of how for Jean, love always meant disaster. She went on—

"I came to believe," she told the friend, "that it was my destiny that never would I find happiness in love, as other women do. I was even told so by mystics, astrologers.

This is the last photograph of the beautiful star and was taken during the final scenes of Saratoga, an M-G-M film in which she was starred with Clark Gable

'Happiness in marriage—you were never born for it. For you, it is forbidden,' they said. I've come to believe it.
"But somehow, it's changed since I've known Bill . . ."

She went on then, with her heart-revelations. Told this young man, who knew Bill, too, what a wonderful fellow Powell is, and how he brought to her the things she'd never found before—a keen-witted mental companionship, a friendship that is the essential part of a true love between man and woman, an understanding and a tolerance that she'd never known from a man before.

Yet, as she told it, there was little happiness in Jean's voice. "It was," the man told me, "as if she felt the doom that overhung her newfound happiness." And at last she said the words I've repeated above— " . . . *when it ends, as it probably must . . .*"

"I thought," her confidante told me sadly, as Jean lay dead, "that it was maybe the cynicism of Hollywood that was speaking—that she meant only that, like so many other Hollywood 'romances,' it couldn't last. But now I know she meant—this. She knew that Death was going to rob her of the happiness that had been always denied her."

YET remember—you who loved Jean Harlow— Jean herself, even in that realization, felt that instead of having been cheated, she had, in the final balance, outwitted her unhappy destiny. For in the months of her companionship and happiness with Bill Powell — even though it never came to marriage—she found a full measure of joy. A measure that, in her own words, balanced all the unhappiness that had been hers until then.

And remember, that at the moment she died, the person who was closest to her in that hospital chamber of death was Bill Powell himself. At the final swing of the scythe that cut short that gorgeous but so-young life, the man with whom she'd learned the real meaning of love, was holding her hand.

Bill doesn't know—won't, until he reads this—how happy Jean was with him, and how utterly his love made up to Jean for everything else. He doesn't know, perhaps, that because of the love she found with him, Jean Harlow in the shadow of death was no longer the "child of sorrow" but instead, was happy—and content.

Bibliographic sources :

Hollywood (1934-1943)

Publisher: Hollywood Magazine, inc. ; Fawcett Publications, inc.

www.ingramcontent.com/pod-product-compliance
Lightning Source LLC
Chambersburg PA
CBHW020955180526
45163CB00006B/2381